DEAR FOLKS at HOME

DEAR FOLKS at HOME

Letters of Eugene H. Sackett, Philippine Campaign,
May 30, 1898 to September 22, 1899

Russell H. Sackett, compiler

PALMETTO
PUBLISHING
Charleston, SC
www.PalmettoPublishing.com

Copyright © 2025 by Russell H. Sackett

All rights reserved

No portion of this book may be reproduced, stored in a retrieval system, or transmitted in any form by any means–electronic, mechanical, photocopy, recording, or other–except for brief quotations in printed reviews, without prior permission of the author.

Hardcover ISBN: 9798822977846
Paperback ISBN: 9798822977853
eBook ISBN: 9798822977860

Dedicated to my Aunt Mary Sackett
who passed her father's letters to me.

Contents

Table of Figures ix
Introduction xiii
The First North Dakota Infantry 1
    Official History of the Operations of the First North Dakota
    Infantry, U.S.V. in the Campaign I the Philippine Islands 2
    To Santa Cruz 8
    A Masonic Military Lodge 23
Camp Merrit, San Francisco 27
Transport to Manila, Philippine Islands 49
Letters From Manila—Camp Inartel de Malatee 60
Letters From Manila—Inland Campaign 118
Letters From Manila—Hospital and Transport Home 179
After the War 193
References 195

Table of Figures

Fig. 1: The Hottest of the Fight, Battle of Manila Bay. xi
Fig. 2: The "Raleigh"—this Gun Crew fired the first shot in Manila Bay. xi
Fig. 3: The Nation's Hero-Admiral Dewey on his Flagship "Olympia,"
Manila Bay xii
Fig. 4: Ft. Malate shelled by Dewey, Aug. 13, '98 xiv
Fig. 5: Eugene Hayward Sackett, ca. 1901 xvi
Fig. 6: Camp of the American Army at Manila, Philippines. 4
Fig. 7: Major General Henry Lawton | after a hard day of campaigning
in the Philippine Islands. 9
Fig. 8: Resting by the wayside, Lawton's Expedition. 9
Fig. 9: Philippine Islands Campaign, 1899–1901 20
Fig. 10: Stricken with Fever—more deadly than Filipino bullets—
1st Reserve Hospital, Manila, Philippine Islands. 22
Fig. 11: Floor Plan of North Dakota Military Lodge Home of Masons,
Manila, P.I. Drawing by Eugene H. Sackett 24
Fig. 12: Front and Side Elevations of North Dakota Military Lodge
Home of Masons, Manila, P.I. Drawing by Eugene H. Sackett 25
Fig. 13: Train to Sutro Baths. 51st Iowa camp on the left, Lone Mountain
in the distance, and South Dakota Army on right. Summer 1898.
From the Park Archives Collections, Golden Gate National Recreation Area,
National Park Service, No. PAM Photo Prints, Box 3, F.62. 30
Fig. 14: Camp Merritt, Summer 1898. From the Photo Collections of
Golden Gate National Recreation Area, National Park Service,
No. GOGA-2418, Dan Reese-Camp Merritt Photo Collection.. 31
Fig. 15: Pay Day in the Army. 33
Fig. 16: "Cease Firing!"—Co. F, 1st Colorado Infantry, U.S. Volunteers,
Camp Merritt, San Francisco, CA. 34
Figure 17: Leaving the Presidio, San Francisco, to embark for Manila. 47
Fig. 18: Transport "Pennsylvania" leaving San Francisco with Thirteen

Hundred Volunteers for Manila 48
Fig. 19: U.S. Troops leaving San Francisco for Manila...................... 48
Fig. 20: A Thousand Boys in Blue on S.S. Rio-de Janeiro bound for Manila 48
Fig. 21: Executive Palace, Honolulu, Hawaiian Island. Strohmeyer & Wyman Publishers, N.Y.. 54
Fig. 22: Wreckage of Spanish Ship, Manila Bay, Philippine Islands............ 59
Fig. 23: Envelop from Eugene Sackett with drawing of ships in Manila Bay..... 61
Fig. 24: United States Monitor "Monterey" 63
Fig. 25: Gateway through the Parpeted Wall of Old Manila—entrance from Caile Nueva-Philippines 63
Fig. 26: Old Spanish Battery—Luneta, Manila 64
Fig. 27: Modern Spanish Battery on Luneta, Manila.......................... 64
Fig. 28: Looking Northwest from Tower of the Church of Ronondo, Manila, Philippine Islands.. 65
Fig. 29: Rosario Street and Binondo Church, from the Pasiq River, Manila, Philippine Islands.. 66
Fig. 30: Escolta, the principal business street in Manila, Philippine Islands..... 66
Fig. 31: The Beautiful Church of San Sebastian-built of steel, Manila, Philippine Islands. 66
Figure 32: This is taken in "Calle Real" or Real Avenue, near our quarters..... 86
Fig. 33: Envelop by Eugene Sackett....................................... 105
Fig. 34: Nebraska Out-post attached by Filipinos........................... 119
Fig. 35: Montana Boys on Out-post duty, P.I. 120
Fig. 36: U.S. "Monadnock" in Mary Island Dry Dock, California. Strohmeyer and Wyman, Publishers, N.Y. 122
Fig. 37: The Palace—Headquarters of Maj. Gen. Otis—Manila, Philippine Islands 124
Fig. 38: North Dakota Volunteers quartered in the Old Church at Paete, San Antonio, P.I. Photographed and Published by B. W. Kilburn, Littleton, N. H.... 126
Fig. 39: Expecting a Filipino Attach behind the Cemetery Wall, Pasig, Phil, Is'ds.. 127

Table of Figures

Fig. 40: Fighting line near Pasay—the Trenches and Lookout Guard, Philippine Islands 129

Fig. 41: 14th regiment fighting from captured Filipino Trenches in the woods near Pasa[y, P.I. 130

Fig. 42: A Sixth Artillery Gatling Gun driving Insurgents out of the brush, Pasay, P.I. 131

Figure 43: North Dakota Volunteers in Camp at San Antonio, P.I. Photographed and Published by B. W. Kilburn, Littleton, N. H. 132

Fig. 44: The Heliograph Station—ignaling between land and naval forces— near Pasay, P.I. 132

Fig. 45: The Sixth Artillery watching the effect of their Shells, Pasay, Philippine Islands 133

Fig. 46: The 14th Infantry entrenched at Pasay, P.I. 134

Fig. 47: Commissary Station, San Fernando, P.I. 139

Figure 48: The Insurgent House of Congress on Fire Matolos, P.I. Photographed and Published by B. W. Kilburn, Littleton, N. H. 147

Fig. 49: Reinforcements going to the front, P.I. 157

Figure 50: Resting by the way, Lawton's expedition, P.I. Photographed and Published by B. W. Kilburn, Littleton, N. H. 162

Fig. 51: Interior of Santa Ana Church—our field Hospital during the fight— Philippines 165

Fig. 52: Filipino Buffaloes—hauling Water to the Front—San Pedro Macati, Philippines. 167

Fig. 53: On the march 168

Figure 54: The prison where the insurgents kept the fourteen American Prisoners. Drawing by Eugene H. Sackett. 172

Figure 55: A Morning Ride in a Jinrikisha, Sugita, Japan Strohmeyer & Wyman, Publishers, New York, N.Y. 187

Figure 56: Visit to Yokohama, Japan, on the way home. 190

Fig. 57: Welcome home button. 191

Fig. 58: Eugene Hayward Sackett and family, ca. 1914. 193

Introduction

Commodore George Dewey issued the command to open fire on the Spanish fleet in Manila Bay on May 1, 1889, at quarter to six in the morning. A short seven hours later, the Spanish Pacific fleet lay destroyed. Dewey's fleet did not suffer any damage during the engagement.[1]

FIGURE 1: The Hottest of the Fight, Battle of Manila Bay.

FIGURE 2: The "Raleigh"—this Gun Crew fired the first shot in Manila Bay.

---

1 Karnow, Stanley *In Our Image: America's Empire in The Philippines*. New York: Ballantine Books. 1898. p.78.

The United States declared war on Spain April 26, 1898. In anticipation of this conflict, Dewey was sent to Hong Kong to take command of the U.S. Asiatic Squadron with instruction that once hostilities broke out between the U.S. and Spain the fleet was to proceed to Manila and destroy Spain's Pacific Fleet. Intent of this engagement was to deny Spain the ability to harass the west coast of the United States. This action allowed war efforts to focus on Cuba and Puerto Rico.

The purpose of the action in Manila was not part of a larger military plan to take the Philippine Islands. It was to deny Spain's ability to poise a threat to the United State in the Pacific. Dewey did not have enough men under his command to take the Philippines.[2]

FIGURE 3: The Nation's Hero-Admiral Dewey on his Flagship "Olympia," Manila Bay.

At the time of the engagement, Spain was fighting an uprising in the Philippines. This uprising against their rule began years before the Spanish American War. By 1898, the Filipinos had confined the presents of Spain to Manila and a few other large towns. Manila was under siege. The Filipinos saw the United States as a liberator. A clause in the Declaration of War, insisted on by Congress, directed the United States to withdraw from

---

2 Trask, David F. *The War with Spain in 1898.* Lincoln: University of Nebraska Press. 1981 p.382.

Cuba once hostilities ceased and a free Cuban government formed led the Filipinos that the same policy would apply to the Philippine Islands.

With the Spanish fleet destroyed and Dewey unable to take Manila, a void in the power structure developed. Other nations interested in global expansion, such as Japan and Germany, sent ships to the Philippines to observe. At one point, the German fleet out-gunned Dewey and poised a threat. Intervention by the British fleet in assisting Dewey caused the German fleet to withdraw a few of its ships. In part due to these international pressures, President McKinley decided to provide the forces needed to take the Philippine Islands. President McKinley decided that the United States should replace Spain in the Philippines.[3]

When war was declared with Spain, McKinley had called for a force of 124,000 volunteers. However, with the President's decision to extend army operations to include the Philippines, more volunteers were required. On May 25th a second call for volunteers was issued for an additional 75,000 men.

Forces adequate to take Manila were placed under the Command of General Merritt by August 1898. Negotiating with the Spanish Governor- General, Don Fermin Jaudenses y Alavarez, Dewey and Merritt arranged to have a sham battle for the Spanish to save face prior to surrendering the city. The negotiations selected Fort San Antonio Abad at Malate to be shelled by Dewey's fleet on August 13, 1898. This was followed by Merritt's forces marching and taking Manila. The sham battle was also to allow the U.S. forces to take control of Manila before the Filipino rebels had time to react. This action began the mistrust between the Filipino fighters and the United States. This continued to escalate until hostilities broke out on February 4, 1899 to mark the beginning of the Filipino-American War.

---

3 Smith, Joseph. *The Spanish-American War: Conflict in the Caribbean and the Pacific 1895–1902*. London: Longman. 1994, p.222.

FIGURE 4: Ft. Malate shelled by Dewey, Aug. 13, '98

By the close of the Filipino-American War on July 4, 1902, over 126,000 American troops served in the Philippines. Of this number, over 4,000 were killed and 2,000 wounded. Between 16,000 and 20,000 insurgents died in the conflict with an additional estimated 200,000 civilian deaths. The conflict delivered a damaging blow to the United States' international image as a nation dedicated to freedom and democracy.[4]

Eugene Sackett wrote the following letters while serving in the North Dakota Volunteers in the Philippine Islands. Eugene burned the letters written to him towards the end of his stay. Maps and drawings prepared by him and mentioned in his letters are no longer in the family. These were placed in a Fargo store window for the community to see and keep up with the hometown company. These may still exist in various archives.

These letters appear as Eugene wrote them. They begin May 30, 1898 describing his railroad trip from Fargo, North Dakota to Camp Merrit, San Francisco, California and end September 22, 1899 with his return to San Francisco. Eighty-one letters compose the collection.

The letters fall into five broad categories that describe the various stages of his stay in the army. The first group consists of 14 letters that

---

[4] Smith, Joseph. *The Spanish-American War: Conflict in the Caribbean and the Pacific 1895–1902*. London: Longman. 1994, p.225.

date from May 30, 1898 to June 28, 1898. These were written while at Camp Merrit and deal with how life was as a Company Clerk, the camp itself, prices the government charged for clothing and equipment, quality of foods supplied, ships being built at the Navy Yard; fortifications around San Francisco; San Francisco; and sickness brought about by his vaccination becoming infected. The blue dye of the uniform infected the arm.

Two letters dating July 3, 1898 and July 24, 1898 represent the next series. These deal with the trip from San Francisco to Manila on board the transport *S.S. Valencia*. The letters address what Honolulu was like and the reception held for the soldiers, life on the transport and close loss of his arm due to infection.

The third set of letters (26 letters) date from August 19, 1898 to January 1, 1899. These are ones written while in Manila. This period represents relative inactivity militarily. The letters deal with life for the soldiers in the city, descriptions of the quarters they lived in, costs of living in Manila, food, guard duty and the outposts manned by the volunteers. This period was inactive as far as campaigning and Eugene discusses the boredom of the soldiers, activities to keep them busy and the constant waiting for the mail ships.

The fourth set of letters (23 letters) date from January 13, 1899 to June 2, 1899. Eugene wrote these from various locations. The letters represent the period that Eugene's company actively campaigned against the Insurgents. These go into detail about the fighting out of Manila, the campaigns into the inland regions, food supplies, general life of the soldiers, etc. This set of letters end with Eugene contracting yellow fever.

The final set of 16 letters covers a period from June 12, 1899 to September 22, 1899. This set covers Eugene's confinement in the hospital, the trip back to San Francisco and a little bit about his stay in that city before leaving for home in Fargo, North Dakota.

I am indebted to my Aunt Mary who faithfully kept the letters and other memorabilia brought back from the Philippine Islands by my grandfather. The letters, more than anything, provides a window to a family member and an insight into conditions that an individual lived under during the War of 1898. The original letters are now part of the Park Archives Collections, Golden Gate National Recreation Area, National Park Service.

FIGURE 5: Eugene Hayward Sackett, ca. 1901

The First North Dakota Infantry

To set a context to interpret the letters the following is a recopy of the "Official History of the Operations of the First North Dakota Infantry, U.S.V. in the Campaign I the Philippine Islands" written by First Sergeant Phillip H. Shortt in 1899.[5] The figures inserted in the text are not original to it. This is not a history of the War of 1898. The following books provide a more complete understanding of the war. *Campaigning in the Philippines* by Karl Irving Faust (published in 1899 by the Hicks-Judd Company Publishers of San Francisco) provides a detailed history of the war in the Philippines starting with the navel battle in Manila Bay and ending in the summer of 1899 with the replacement of the "Volunteer Army" by the Regular Army. This book only discusses the events and does not address the whys. *The Mirror of War: American Society and The Spanish American War* by Gerald F. Linderman (published in 1974 by The University of Michigan Press, Ann Arbor, Michigan) is recommended to understand why the Spanish American War occurred. In this same vain, *Flood Tide of Empire: Span and the Pacific Northwest, 1543–1819* by Warren L. Cook (published in 1973 by Yale University Press, New Haven, Connecticut) is recommended to understand the decline of the Spanish Empire and why she was a logical candidate for a maturing United States to test her strength against. Finally, *The Spanish War: An American Epic—1898* by G.J.A. O'Toole (published in 1984 by the W.W. Norton & Company, New York, New York) is recommend for a complete history of the war.

---

5 Shortt, First Sergeant Phil. H. "Official History of the Operations of the First North Dakota Infantry, U.S.V. in the Campaign in the Philippine Islands." In *Campaigning in the Philippines* by Karl Irving Faust, Supplemental pages 1–19. San Francisco: The Hicks-Judd Company. 1899

Official History of the Operations of the First North Dakota Infantry, U.S.V. in the Campaign I the Philippine Islands[6]

When the call for troops came after the declaration of war, in the early spring of 1898, the National Guard of the State of North Dakota was not in the best condition. It had been nearly five years since an encampment had been held, and active interest in National Guard affairs was kept up only by a few of the most enthusiastic National Guardsmen of the State. On the 26th of April, 1898, when the Governor issued orders to rendezvous the First Regiment at Fargo, the call found nearly every company filled to maximum-eighty-one enlisted men. The short space of time required to raise the number of men required to more than doubly fill the State's quota was remarkable. Owing to the fact that some states were not so prompt in filling their quotas as was the State of North Dakota, the War Department decided to utilize the two battalions mobilized at Faro in their entirely.

It was on the 2d of May, 1898, that the regiment assembled at Camp Briggs, Fargo, and, as a whole, they were poorly equipped in all military supplies. Arms in sufficient numbers were unobtainable, many men were ununiformed, and several companies had to sleep in the armory, as there were not sufficient tents to shelter the command. Out of all this confusion and lack of material, in an incredibly short time, as it seemed to all, the battalions emerged as the First North Dakota Volunteer Infantry, a regiment of excellent appearance and discipline.

The eight different cities and towns in which companies forming the regiment were recruited are as follows: Bismarck, Company A; Fargo, Company B; Grafton, Company C; Devil's Lake, Company D; Valley City, Company G: Jamestown, Company H; Wahpeton, Company I, and Dickinson, Company K.

---

6 Excerpt from *Campaigning in the Philippines*... by Karl Irving Faust. Copyrighted 1899 by The Hicks-Jud Company, Saf Francisco, Cal.

From the 2d to the 26th of May, this raw material was worked upon and drilled in the manual, squad and platoon movements, evolutions of the company and battalion and skirmish drill, and when, on the later date, the regiment left for San Francisco it was a well-drilled and disciplined lot of men.

The trip to San Francisco was made over the Northern Pacific by the companies of the first battalion, while the second battalion and headquarters went over the Great Northern. The journey was a delightful one, occurring just at the time of year when the mountains and plains are re-clothed in beautiful verdure, and the journey was one continuous ovation.

Arriving in San Francisco on June 1, 1898, it was as though the whole city had turned out to greet the incoming troops. The reception accorded to the regiment was a pleasant one, and the hospitality shown on its advent was fully equaled by the displayed throughout its four weeks' stay in the charming California metropolis. On June 27th, the First North Dakota went on board the steamer *Valencia*, the streets on the way to the steamer being filled with people who bade the regiment hearty farewells and wished it success and good luck. The scene at the wharf was beyond description. The docks were crowded with soldiers, and the ladies of the Red Cross were everywhere conspicuous. Flowers, fruit and all sorts of refreshments were tendered the boys bound for Manila.

The North Dakota Regiment was the last to leave of the regiments of the third expedition, but the *Valencia* overtook the balance of the other boats forming the expedition at Honolulu, and the voyage from that port on was made in goodly company. The stay at Honolulu was shortened by the lateness of departure from San Francisco, but all heartily enjoyed their brief visit to that city, and the boys did ample justice to the bountiful dinner servered to them in the palace grounds. The voyage was a pleasant one throughout, aside form the attending and unavoidable discomforts to be found on any crowded troopship, and the weather was exceptionally fine.

The expedition arrive in Manila bay on the 30th day of July, 1898, and the North Dakotas reported but one man of the regiment on the sick list, Lieutenant Conklin, who had fever, and was admitted to the hospital at Cavite. The regiment was disembarked at Cavite on the 5th day of August, 1898, and after a few days in quarters there, on the 9th, the regiment took the position assigned to it at Camp Dewey, with the balance of the besieging forces in front of Manila.

FIGURE 6: Camp of the American Army at Manila, Philippines

Only a few days afterward, the city yielded, after a brief conflict with the American forces, and the regiment's experience in the Spanish-American war was brought to a close. The North Dakotas were in MacArthur's column at the battle of Manila, and only one member of the regiment, Private Berg, of Company A, was wounded in this engagement.

The first few days after arriving in the city were anxious ones. Aguinoldo's followers threatened to burn and loot the city, and it seemed at one time that a contest must immediately result between them and the American forces. Companies C and K were in a perilous position guarding the Paco bridge on the night of the 13th, and Company A at the Puente de Ayala, were also hard pressed, but the trouble was fortunately averted for the time.

On the 16th of August, the regiment was permanently quartered in the Nipa barracks on the Calle Real, Malate, just opposite the Cuartel de Malate.

The next six months, up to the night of February 4, 1899, were monotonous repetitions; each, of the one just preceding it. Barrack life, guard and outpost duty, steady, patient drill, brightened by the days when mail came form the states, made up the life led. It was tiresome, but of benefit. When the outbreak came, in place of raw levies, there were veteran troops, ready for any duty and at any time.

The strain had been gradually getting tenser each day and when the uprising occurred on the night of February 4, 1899, everybody breathed a sigh of relief.

On the night of February 4th, one company of the regiment, Company I, was doing outpost duty at the Singalon Church. The balance of the regiment was in barracks, and when the call to arms came they promptly formed in the streets in front of their quarters and moved down and occupied the trenches just south of Fort San Antonio de Abad, as well as the fort itself.

There was no firing on this front until just at daybreak, but the sound of the conflict seemed to creep along form the extreme left of the line, gradually getting plainer and plainer, till at dawn the rebels opened fire all along the south front. The fire was a hot one and was returned with interest until about 10 a.m., when Lieutenant-Colonel Treumann ordered a charge on the rebel trenches, and Major Frank White, with Companies G, H ad D, made a most brilliant charge across the rice fields, a distance of some 300 yards, driving the enemy in the direction of the Old American Camp Dewey. This cleared the enemy away from that immediate front. Many of the insurgents lost their lives in this combat, and so rapidly did the North Dakotans advance that some insurrectos were captured in their trenches. During the night of the 4th and the morning of the 5th, Company I was hotly engaged near Blockhouse 12 and in support of a battery at Blockhouse 13, not joining the regiment until the next day.

At 3 P.M. on Sunday, February 5th, the regiment left their trenches, driving the enemy, already badly demoralized, in the direction of

Pasay. The left of the line connected with the Fourteenth Infantry, and the right rested on the shore of the bay. At Pasay major White's battalion, with Company D, was moved in the direction of San Pedro Macati, and marched up on the hills overlooking that town, and Major Fraine's battalion took up a line from the beach at Pasay. Colonel Treumann established regimental headquarters on the beach and kept up a signal communication with the fleet, one vessel of which was anchored about a mile and a half off shore.

The day had been a fortunate one for the regiment-for not a man had been injured during all that heavy fire. It had also shown the material of which the men were composed, and officers and men were proud of the fact that they belonged to the First North Dakota.

On the 6th of February, Major Fraine, with Companies I and K, made a reconnaissance toward Paranaque, proceeding as far south as the Paranaque River and obtaining specific information as to the location of the enemy and drawings of his trenches. After the purpose of the reconnaissance had been accomplished, the companies returned to their positions on the line.

The order was at this time received to entrench the position held by our lines, and the boys ere introduced to a fine new lot of spaces, picks, etc., furnished by the quartermaster. Many were the works of grief indulged in, as day after day the boys dug in the sand or gumbo, building a line of breastworks between the beach and a point nearly a mile east of Pasay; trenches that were held for days, under a more or less constantly dropping fire form the insurgents, but not direct attack. The insurgents had gotten past the time when they assailed Americans entrenched.

On the 10th of February, the report again came that the rebels were massing on the south line, in front of the position held by the North Dakotas, Fourteenth Infantry and Fourth Cavalry. Once more Companies K and I, in company with detachments from the Fourteenth Infantry and Fourth Cavalry, visited the banks of the Paranaque River, remaining there till an early hour the following morning, being withdrawn to Pasay just before daybreak. The next month was all in all an uneventful one, an occasional brush between the outposts furnishing an occasional few moments' diversion.

On the 14th of March, Colonel Treumann received orders to report to General Charles King at San Pedro Macati with his command. The next day the regiment moved out of San Pedro t points along the river and Malabay Road, guarding the line of communication between San Pedro and the points occupied by the Washington Regiment Pasig, Taguig and Pateros and keeping the river and the road skirting its banks free from the enemy.

During the three weeks that ensued, there were several brushes between our outposts and the enemy, the most important of which was the engagement which took place April 1st, at a point almost due south of San Pedro. General King ordered Major White to drive in a strong outpost, estimated at between two and three hundred, of the enemy. The scouts had located the post, as well as a trail which enabled the troops to get within close range before their presence could be discovered. Two companies, A, Captain Moffett, and D, Captain Cogswell, formed the firing line, with the balance of the command in easy supporting distance. Just at daybreak the ball opened, the advance having been made to within a couple of hundred yards under cover of the darkness. The enemy stubbornly fought to hold their position, but in vain. The rapid and well-aimed fire of the Americans soon drove them out of their trenches and they retreated with confusion and loss across an open filed to a line of bamboo. They lost heavily during their retrograde movement. In this skirmish, Lieutenant D. Baldwin, Jr., First Battalion Adjutant, was wounded in the right leg below the knee, while advancing at the head of the men; Private E. Morgan, of Company D, received a slight wound inn the forehead and Corporal John C. Byron, of Company D, received a would which resulted in his death, May 24, 1899.

To Santa Cruz

On the 8th day of April, 1899, Major John H. Fraine of the Second Battalion, was ordered to join the first expedition to the lake country under General Lawton.

The troops comprising this command consisted of two battalions of the Fourteenth Infantry, one battalion of the First Idahos, three troops of the Fourth Cavalry, Hawthorne's Mountain Battery, and the second battalion, North Dakotas. The troops were all picked for the trip, and on the afternoon of the 8th were towed in cascoes up the Pasig River to the lake. It was a beautiful trip, and one which will linger long in the memories of the men who made it. The beautiful Pasig River, the broad expanse of lake, shaded by the mountain, all caught the eye and held the fancy. This section of the Island of Luzon is picturesque in the extreme. Far across the waters of the Laguna de Bay gleamed the white domes and towers of a hundred churches, beauties, and showed the members of the expedition a land full of promise but where the American had never been; a land full of dangers, both from savage foes and from exposures incident to the climatic conditions.

The first encounter with the enemy occurred on the evening of the 9th. The troops had been successfully landed under the protecting fire of the gunboats *Laguna de Bay, Napindan* and *Oeste,* and the line deployed in beautiful order, all the troops in line except the Fourth Cavalry. The brisk skirmish that followed was effected in clearing our immediate front of the enemy, the Fourteenth and Idahos taking the leading part in the combat. The firing cased just at dusk, and the members of the various commands retired to rest. The rice fields were neither smooth nor soft, but the men were tired and, without a thought of the morrow's dangers, sank to sleep.

FIGURE 7: Major General Henry Lawton after a hard day of campaigning in the Philippine Islands.

FIGURE 8: Resting by the wayside, Lawton's Expedition.

Long before daybreak on the morning of April 10th, the command was on the alert, and just at dawn the advance was ordered. The Fourth Cavalry made a hearty attack upon the front of the insurgent trenches, supported by the gunboats, while the balance of the troops swung in upon the left and rear of the enemy. The advance was a beautiful sight, the troops moving up steadily in the face of a brisk fire, crossing the river and driving the enemy through the town and out into the rice fields beyond. It was at this point that the heaviest loss was inflicted upon the rebels. The fire of the gunboats was hot and fierce, and the infantrymen poured a heavy fire into the enemy, who were in full flight. The loss inflicted was heavy, over three hundred being killed, wounded or taken prisoners by our forces. The expedition spent the day in Santa Cruz, as well as the ensuing night.

On the early morning of the 11th the start was made for Pagsangjan. This is a beautiful city, situated on the Caviente River, and is the most delightful place that the writer has visited on the island of Luzon. The soil is wonderfully fertile, and the whole surrounding country shows evidence of great prosperity. There are mammoth forests of cocoanut and banana trees, and all the fruits indigenous to the island grow in profusion. The movement toward this place and its capture was accomplished with almost no opposition, the enemy being completely demoralized by their losses of the preceding day.

It was at Pagsangjan that the North Dakotas captured Aguinoldo's so-called navy, consisting of seven steam launches and two sailing cascoes. Two good steam launches were found tied up right at the town, while the balance of the boats were over a mile up stream, moored to the opposite bank. The capture of these boats was one of the principal objects of the expedition, as their loss rendered communication between the insurgent forces in the north and south of the island extremely difficult. The work of the regiment was characterized by the Adjutant-General of the division, who was present, as a most brilliant proceeding. Volunteers were called to swim the river in the face of a heavy expected fire; they responded promptly, and received honorable mention for their gallantry.

A night's rest at Pagsangjan and the second battalion started out for Paete, the balance of the command followed. After crossing the Cavienete River, the march followed a road which winds along the lake shore, at the base of the high hills skirting the lake at this point. On entering a part of the roadway where the cliffs seemed to tower right over our heads, the sound of the Mauser was heard in our front. The sharpshooters had been detailed to act as the advance guard of the column, and they had been fired on. One squad, that of Company C, had been almost wiped out, four out of the five men constituting the squad being killed. The fire was a very brisk one for a few minutes, and as soon as the column could be deployed into line it was returned with interest. Half of the battalion advanced up the hill in splendid order, firing platoon volleys at short distances, clearing the woods of the enemy and driving them along the hills into and past Pueblo de Paete. The balance of the command remained in the road below as support. When about half way up the hill the line made a left turn, and advanced right along the hills parallel with the road. It was a hard journey, through tangled undergrowth and vines, over rocks, and sliding along the face of a precipitous hill. The enemy retired, and as they left the town the gunboats opened at them and completed their demoralization

After the first fire, the insurgent bugles sounded their bolo charge, but the fire of the Dakotans was too warm, and next sounded "retreat," which was promptly obeyed. The regiment lost five men killed and two seriously wounded. Of these, four were from Company C, and were members of the sharpshooters. This squad was to the extreme right of the advance, and after the first volley Private Thomas Sletteland was the only man left alive. He coolly took up a good position and covered the bodies of his comrades with his rifle, keeping the enemy from securing their rifles and ammunition belts. He has been recommended for a medal of honor for his daring deed.

The five killed in this brief action were: Corporal Isador Driscoll, Waggoner Peter Tompkins, Privates Alfred C. Almen and William G. Lamb, all of company C, and Musician George Schneller, of Company I. Privates Herbert C. Files, of Company I, and August Heusel, of Company K, were seriously wounded, but have recovered.

Taking into consideration all the natural advantages of troops fighting upon the defensive in such a location, it seems strange that the loss inflicted was not much heavier. The Chinamen and natives informed the writer that it was in this very pass that the Seventy-third Spanish Regiment of the line was almost annihilated but a very few years ago.

The night of April 12th, the battalion was quartered in the picturesque old church of the Pueblo de Paete, where it remained for three days. At the end of this time the expedition, having accomplished its purpose, returned to Manila, the part of the North Dakotas engaged landing at San Pedro, taking up their old position on the Malabay Road.

Three days later, on the 19th of April, the regiment was ordered into their Malate barracks to make preparations for an expedition with General Lawton to San Miguel. On the afternoon of April 21st, with ten days' rations, the regiment marched out to La Loma Church, where they went into camp near the Third and Twenty-second Regiments, regular infantry, Scott's Battery of the Sixth Artillery and Hawthorne's Mountain Battery, Fourth Cavalry, and these troops, with the Thirteenth Minnesota and Second Oregons, under Colonel Somers of the Second Oregon formed Lawton's expedition to the north line.

April 22d, the column moved northeast, into the enemy's country, Lieutenant Colonel Treumann commanding the brigade, the North Dakotas in advance, under command of Major White. After moving about six miles in the direction of Novaleches, the First Battalion, under command of Major Frank White, first encountered the enemy. Company H, under Captain Eddy, was in the extreme advance and was in some warm work for a few minutes, until the balance of the battalion deployed, with Companies A and G on the left of Company H, and Company B on the right of that company, while Company I of the Second battalion formed the extreme right of the line. The pace was a warm one, and the enemy broke for the hills before the steady, determined advance of the Dakotas. After arriving within a mile of Novaleches, the enemy again made a show of resistance. The First Battalion was again deployed, and, after the crossing of the river had been effected under fire, advanced to and through the town of Novaleches, driving the insurgents and inflicting some loss. In this engagement Corporal Hansche of Company B was seriously, and Private Fell of Company I was slightly wounded. The column stopped for the night at Novaleches.

The few days that followed were more full of hardships than any others encountered by the regiment. The weather was terribly hot, and the water supply extremely poor. The transportation train consisted of carts drawn by caribous, and these poor beasts were driven frantic for want of water, many dying by the wayside, the men of this regiment drawing the carts and loads where the bulls had died or played out. The roads were mere trails and the country was not well known, and Spanish maps were not reliable. The men were worn out pulling the provision carts up one hill and letting them down the next by means of long ropes, and progress was extremely slow. Some days it was impossible to make more than three miles. The hills were high and steep, and every little water—course had almost perpendicular banks. The country was practically treeless and the troops suffered a great deal. On the night of April 24th the troops camped at San Jose del Monte, and on the 26th they arrived at Angat, which had been destroyed the previous day by the Oregon and Minnesota Regiments, under command of Colonel Somers. General Lawton's expedition consisted of two columns. The one under Colonel Somers, composed of parts of the Thirteenth Minnesota, Second Oregon and Hawthorne's Battery, came by a parallel road, leaving the railway at Bocane, arrived at Angat a day ahead of the other column, having good roads all the way.

It was at Angat that Civilian W.H. Young organized the small band of scouts that bore his name, which organization, in the language of Major-General H.W. Lawton, accomplished as much in their venturesome journey into the hostile country as any one regiment of his command. These men were picked for their fitness and intrepidity, and were composed of seventeen men from the North Dakota Volunteers, three from the Fourth U.S. Cavalry and five from the Second Oregon. The first volunteers were Glassly and Longfellow, Company A; McIntyre, Luther and Anders, Company B; Warren, Company C; Jenson, Company D; Davis, Christenson and Gauolt, Company G; Downs and Killian, Company H; Boehler and Desmond, Company I; Thomas, Summerfield and Smith, Company K; others joining after were Kinne, Company B; Truelock, Company C; Hussey and Sweeny, Company K, and Ross of Company H, North Dakota Volunteers.

The scouts were ahead of the column at San Rafael, May 1st, Bustos and Balinag, May 2d. May 3d the party made an advance towards Sampalac on the San Maguel Road, driving the enemy about three miles.

On May 4th, General Lawton ordered Young with his men to proceed to the foothills northeast of Balinag for purpose of locating any body of the enemy and destroying certain munitions of war known to be in that vicinity.

On the 10th of May, they returned, having destroyed about 60,000 bushels of rice stored there. May 11th Young was sent to join Somers' Brigade at Maasin, and the next day the scouts, supported by two companies of the Thirteenth Minnesotas, drove the enemy out of San Ildefonse. At this place Truelock of Company C, was wounded.

May 13th, the enemy was driven out of San Miguel by the scouts, twelve of whom were recommended for medals of honor by Colonel Berkheimer, Twenty-eight Infantry, United States Volunteers, Captain Third United States Artillery, for this deed.

In this fight, the brave leader Young, was mortally wounded, and died in the hospital at Manila, May 16th.

Lieutenant Thornton, Second Oregon, then assumed command, and a skirmish was taken part in the Salaccat May 15th.

On May 16th, being some distance in advance of the column, on the road to San Isidreo, Tarbon Bridge was seen to be on fire, eight hundred yards ahead. A heavy fire was received from the First Manila Regulars, Aguinaldo's Crack Regiment, who were intrenched across the river. Advancing in skirmish line, and finding it too deep to ford, a rush was made across the burning bridge, at this time so weakened that Corporal Thomas, of Company K, fell through into the river. The enemy was driven out, and suffered a loss of twelve killed and six wounded, and two prisoners were taken; afterwords sixteen guns were picked up on the field. The scouts suffered a loss of one man killed, Harrington, Company G, Second Oregon. For this action twenty-three men were recommended for medals of honor by Lieutenant J.E. Thornton.

On May 17th, they took part in the fall of San Isidro. On May 20th, while Somers' Brigade was going down the Rio Grande River, the scouts encountered the enemy at San Antonio, out of which place they were driven after a sharp fight. They returned to Manila from Calumpit on May 26th, with the North Dakota Volunteers.

Captain Wm. E. Berkheimer of the Third Artillery, in speaking, in an official report, of one of the daring exploits of these scouts, says:

"On the 13th of May, 1899, certain scouts of Major-General Lawton's command, supported by a battalion of United States Volunteers, the whole amounting to 118 enlisted men, under my orders, encountered the enemy drawn up in line in front of San Miguel de Mayumo, Philippine Islands, in an advantageous position, the right flank resting on a stream, the left on an elevation rendered

secure by a dense thicket, thus forming a front attack. The total strength of the enemy was ascertained subsequently to have been about 600 men, and while the firing was going on with the enemy's deployed line, I carefully scanned the latter and estimated at the time that I contained about 300 men. Without waiting for the supporting battalion to re-enforce them, or be in a position to do so, a squad of ten scouts following their leaders, Civilian W.H. Young and Private James Harrington, Company Gk, Second Oregon, United States Volunteers, one of their number, making twelve altogether, charged the enemy's line, about 150 yards distant, which first wavered and then reluctantly, but completely, gave way, only to be followed up and driven from the city and environs of San Miguel, a place of great importance. Such are the facts. Recalling them, I have to remark that I know of no act of military heroism which rises superior to this. If history contains its record, I know not the page on which it is written. The voices of Young and Private Harrington are hushed in the stillness of the grave, yet at this moment I can hear them cheerily urging the scouts on to this attack. Let their surviving comrades, each and all, receive the rewards appropriate to their deeds of valor."

Civilian Young was killed before San Miguel, and Private Harrington, who succeeded him as chief of the organization, was killed only a few days later, when Lieutenant Thornton, of the Oregons, was assigned to the command. The work that these men accomplished, was a credit alike to themselves and the regiment which they represented. After arriving at Morong, the members of this band of the organization kept up their work, looking over the country in all directions, and their services in this district were only exceeded by their work accomplished on the northern trip. It was during a skirmish near Morong that Private James Killian was killed while acting as leader.

On April 29th, after several days' rest at Angat, the entire force under General Lawton moved down the Rio Grande River toward San Rafael, Colonel Somers' Brigade on the right bank, and Lieutenant-Colonel Treumann's Brigade on the left bank of the stream. The Third Infantry was in advance, with the North Dakotas in support, while the Twenty-Second was the rear guard. The enemy was encountered on approaching San Rafael, the Third was deployed on the firing line, and the First Battalion of the North Dakotas under Major White, took a position on their extreme left. A few volleys were exchanged with the insurgents, when Scott's Battery arrived upon the scene, and the shrapnel soon put the enemy on the run. At this time the Second Battalion was ordered to cross the Rio Grande River and find the column of Colonel Somers, directing him to return to Marnco, as General Lawton received orders by a mounted messenger from General Otis by way of Bocane, to cease offensive operations for a period of two days, owing to certain negotiations then pending with the insurgents. The command reformed and returned to Angat.

At the beginning of the action, while waiting in the road for orders to advance, one man in the Second Battalion, Private Emil Pepke, of Company I, was wounded in the abdomen.

The days were spent in Angat till May 1st, on which date General Lawton began his forward movement toward San Miguel. Negotiations with the insurgents had come to nothing, and had the appearance of sparring for time by the enemy. Our route again took us past San Rafael, and at this point we had a brief skirmish with the enemy. The Second Battalion was on the firing line, under Major Fraine, and sustained no loss. The First

Battalion which was in support had one man wounded, Private Olstad, of Company G, shot through the leg.

On the 2d of May, the command advanced and occupied the important cities of Bustos and Balinag, with the Twenty-second Infantry in advance. The two cities had already been occupied by Young's scouts and the enemy were in full retreat before our advance got within good striking distance.

On the 4th, 5th and 6th of May, the command enjoyed a rest in the quarters of Balinag. The stay was an enjoyable one, and the boys appreciated the needed rest. On the 5th of May, Company C was sent back to Angat to assist in keeping open line of communication to the railroad; and on May a7th, Companies D, I, and K, under Major Fraine, returned to San Rafael, occupying the town with no opposition. These companies remained in San Rafael for a period of three days, at the end of which time they reported to the regiment at Balinag, Company C returning some days later, and here the regiment remained till May 15th.

On May 15th, the command advanced to San Ildefonse, where they camped for the night. It was at Ildefonse that Mr. Young and his men added to their reputation for daring, driving the enemy ahead of them. At this skirmish Private Truelock, of Company C, was wounded in the knee. On the morning of the 16th the command marched into San Miguel, remaining there a portion of the day, pushing on again at 3 P.M. The daring attack by the scouts in the face of an overwhelming fire of the enemy at this place is narrated in previous pages.

After leaving San Miguel the command moved in the direction of San Isidro, an important insurgent stronghold.

On the morning of May 16th, just after the column had gone into camp, an order came from General Lawton to push ahead at once with two battalions of the Twenty-second Infantry, one battalion North Dakota and Scott's Battery, and join Colonel Somers' command near San Isidro, where a battle was expected the next morning. After a hasty supper, the column got under way, Major Fraine's Battery being left as a rear guard with the train. The column arrived at Colonel Somers' camp at mid-night, tired and weary after a long day's march. Next morning, reveille sounded at 3:30 and by five o'clock the entire column was on the march. After marching about three miles, a halt was made at a burned bridge, near a strongly intrenched position of the enemy, which had been captured by the scouts the day before. General Lawton called the officers of the command together and dispositions were made of the troops for an attack upon San Isidro. Colonel Somers was placed in command of the forces which were assigned as follows: The right wing under command of Lieutenant-Colonel Treumann, and composed of Major White's Battalion of the First North Dakotas on the extreme left of the line, and Major Willis' Battalion of the Second Oregon joining it on the left, Scott's Battery in the center of the road, the left wing under Colonel French, composed of two battalions of the Twenty-second Infantry, and a squadron of the Fourth Cavalry, and two battalions of the Thirteenth Minnesota in reserve. The wings were deployed on either side of the road in the form of a V in order to envelop the flanks of the insurgent position, and the line began to move steadily forward with scouts well in advance.

The First Battalion of the North Dakotas on the extreme right of the firing line met with the heaviest opposition. Captain Eddy was in command of a scouting party sent ahead to get an idea of the ground to be gone over, and after passing through a strip of timber, discovered that the enemy was endeavoring to surround a small party of scouts with a strong force. Almost 300 of the enemy swung out in perfect skirmish order from the edge of the timber on the opposite side of the clearing, and unaware of the presence of Captain Eddy and his men. The enemy were about 800 yards distant, and the balance of the North Dakota Battalion was some 150 yards in the rear of the timber. The attempt to flank the American advance brought the insurgents' left within less then 300 yards of the strip of timber, and to this the Dakotas hurried. As soon as the balance of the battalion had arrived on the firing line, the engagement became general, and, after a few minutes' hot work, the enemy was in full retreat, leaving a number of dead and wounded on the field. While the North Dakota Battalion was still hotly engaged with the enemy some tow miles east of San Isidro, having become engaged with the rear of the column of the retreating insurgent forces, the scouts had driven the four remaining sharpshooters out the city and across the river; the church bells were rung, and the left and center of the column, together with the Oregon Battalion, took possession of the town, the left of the line meeting with no opposition. There were no casualties in the regiment, which seems remarkable, as officers and men were greatly exposed.

This skirmish came late in the afternoon and somewhat unexpectedly, and Colonel French, the commanding officer, deemed it advisable to camp on the field rather than making our destination Cabiao in the dark. Strong outposts were put out, and the insurgents did not molest the camp during the night.

After a day at Cabiao, the regiment resumed its march toward Arayat, where it arrived on May 21st, without further adventure. From this point the route to Calumpit led through the beautiful country on the banks of the Rio Grande de Pampanga, through the pueblos of Candaba and Apalit, and on the 25th of May the command arrived at Calumpit, meeting no opposition on the way. May 26th, the regiment was ordered into Manila for a rest, which it had well earned.

The regiment had been in many warm skirmishes, had covered over one hundred miles of ground, over execrable roads, and practically entirely in a hostile country. At the end of this journey, there were more men present for duty than there were when the regiment left Manila. The writer believes that this record is unique.

After several days' rest in Manila, recruiting the strength of the men, and also re-clothing them, the regiment again received marching orders, and reported to Colonel Whalley at San Pedro Macati, on the evening of June 2d. On the following day Colonel Truemann led his regiment up the Pasig River, passing our old quarters near San Nicholas on the way, and halting for the noon rest at the town of Pasig.

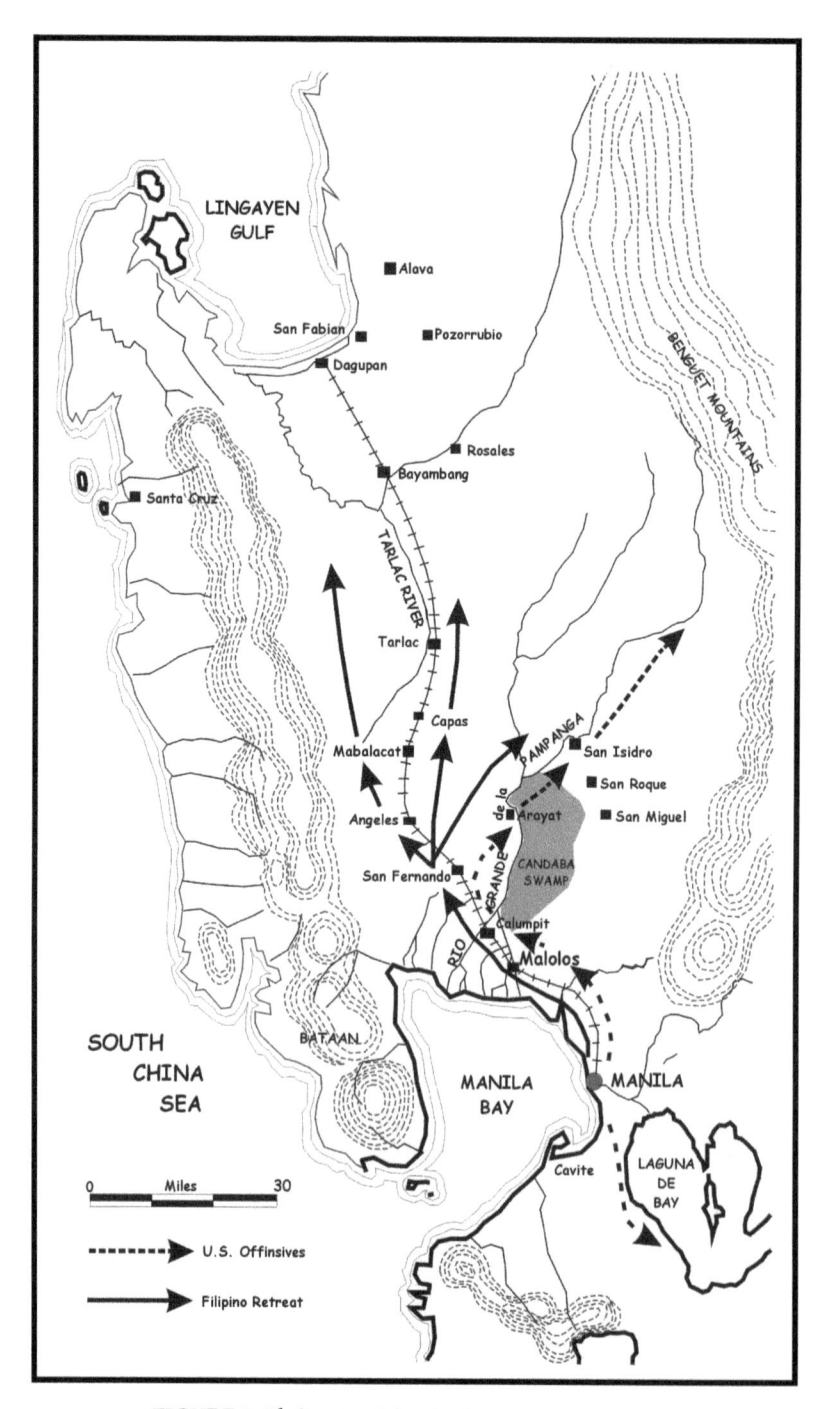

FIGURE 9: Philippine Islands Campaign, 1899–1901

After our mid-day meal, the command consisted of the First Washington Volunteers, two battalions of the Twelth Infantry, the North Dakotas, and portions of two batteries of the Sixth Artillery, started for Cainta and Tay-Tay, where the enemy was reported as being massed in large numbers. The First Washingtons and the Twelth Infantry made the attack upon the town of Cainta from the west. The First North Dakota with one field-piece advanced across the rice fields towards the town of Cainta from the south. The enemy was driven out of Cainta toward Tay-Tay, darkness putting an end to the fighting. The troops camped on the firing line that night. At 5 A.M. Colonel Whalley returned to Pasig, leaving Colonel Truemann in command of the remaining troops. The following morning the town of Tay-Tay was occupied with but little opposition. The enemy had pursued his usual evasive tactics and taken to the hills during the night, leaving the church in a blaze, and the rest of the town stripped bare.

About 10 A.M. the Second Battalion moved out of Tay-Tay in the direction of Antipolo for a distance of nearly three miles, when the advance established connection with General Hall's Brigade and was ordered to return to Tay-Tay. This was a most fatiguing march. More than half of the command were prostrated from heat. After dinner we left the town by another road, skirting the lake shore and going in the direction of Morong, to make a junction with General Hall's Brigade, whose column was moving by road, via Antipolo and Theresa.

The column in command of Lieutenant-Colonel Truemann and consisted of the first North Dakota, two battalions of the Twelfth United States Infantry and Scott's Battery, marched along a road parallel to the lake shore. At Angona, late in the afternoon of June 4th, a small force of the enemy was encountered, but was soon in full retreat. The column passed through a number o villages and the larger pueblos of Binangonan and Cardona. The insurgents had evidently scattered for the hills or changed their uniform for amigo suits of white, hiding their rifles for a more favorable opportunity. But little opposition was met. Arriving at Cardona at 6 P.M., June 5th, a mounted orderly was sent to Morong to communicate with General Hall, Next day, General Hall's Brigade started for Manila over the road which our column had taken, the First Dakota being ordered to proceed to Morong, where the regiment arrived on the 6th, and together with Captain Gale's squadron of the Fourth United States Cavalry, became the garrison for that important city. Frequent skirmishes were had between the insurgent outposts and our scouts, and during one of these Chief of Scouts J.H. Killian, of Company H, was killed. Morong provided a very unhealthy garrison, sickness increasing among the troops at an alarming rate. On the 7th of July, the regiment was relived by six companies of the Twenty-first United States Infantry, under Captain Eltonhead, and returned to Manila on cascoes, after an absence of thirty-five days.

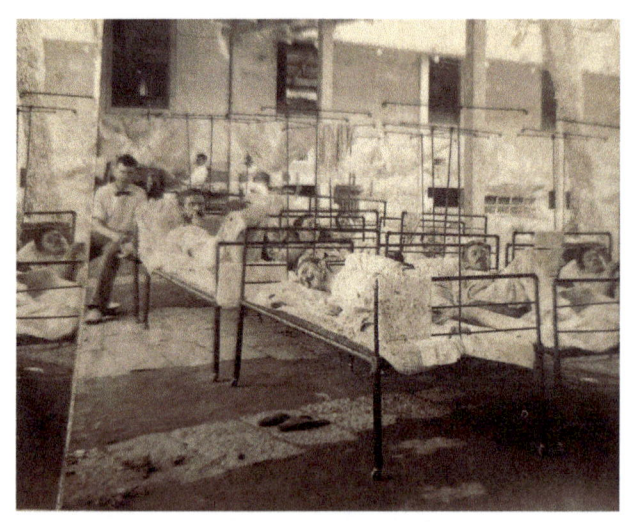

FIGURE 10: Stricken with Fever—more deadly than Filipino bullets—
1st Reserve Hospital, Manila, Philippine Islands

On this date orders were received to prepare the command for embarkation to the United States on the U.S. Transport Grant, and our "Campaigning in the Philippines" may be considered at an end.

During its stay of nearly one year on these islands, the regiment has been in constant contact with the Fourteenth Infantry, the Fourth Cavalry and the First Idahos, ad have been engaged by their side in battles and skirmishes till every member of the regiment feels that no history of this regiment would be complete without a word of commendation extended to these regiments. Uniformly courteaous to the North Dakota men, they have endeared themselves to them by many acts, both of valor and kindness. Comrades, may your days be happy ones in the years to come.

The return voyage form Manila to San Francisco was pleasant, save for the quality of the rations issued on the first part of the voyage. This condition was notably improved, however, after leaving Yokohama, where a fresh supply of vegetables had been laid in. On the 29th of August, the Grant arrived in San Francisco Bay, and on the 31st the eager veterans of the North Dakota Regiment set their foot once more upon American soil. Their reception by the people of San Francisco was a hearty one. The regiment immediately went into camp at the Presidio, and was mustered out of the service of the United States on the 25th of September, 1899.

A Masonic Military Lodge

A portion of the history of the First North Dakota Volunteer Infantry, United States Volunteers, is of peculiar interest to members of the Masonic Order, and in time to come will form part of the Masonic history of the Philippine Islands. While encamped at Fargo, North Dakota, before being ordered to the Philippines it was noticed that a very large number of the officers and men of the regiment were Free Masons, and investigation disclosed the fact that the Lieutenant-Colonel W. C. Truemann commanding the regiment, was Past Master of Crescent Lodge, No. 11, of Grafton, North Dakota, and that Major Frank White, was a Past Senior Warden of Valley City Lodge, No. 7, of Valley City, North Dakota, and Major J. H. Fraine, Junior Warden of Crescent Lodge, No. 11. On suggestion of Brother Frank J. Thompson, Grand Secretary of North Dakota, forty-seven members of the regiment petitioned the Most Worthy for a dispensation permitting the petitioners to meet as Masons when the regiment arrived in a country where Grand Master R.M. Carothers, petition. His action was endorsed by the Grand Lodge when it met, and a dispensation to "Military Lodge, Uniform Degree, of North Dakota," was granted o June 4, 1898, permitting the forty-seven members petitioning therefore, to meet Masonically as a lodge: in the possession of Spain," and empowering the said Lodge to receive as candidates and affiliates such persons connected with the military service of the United States as they should accept.

The first officers named in the dispensation, were Lieutenant-Colonel W. C. Truemann, Worthy Master; Major Frank White, Senior Warden, Major John H. Fraine, Junior Warden. The first meeting of the Lodge was held at No. 79, Calle Real Malate, Manila, Philippine Islands, on August 21, 1898 at 8 P.M. A suitable building was subsequently obtained, and the regular home of the Lodge, when the regiment was in Manila, was the building at No. 69, Calle Nueva Malate, although meetings were held and degrees conferred on the firing line in such buildings as were convenient.

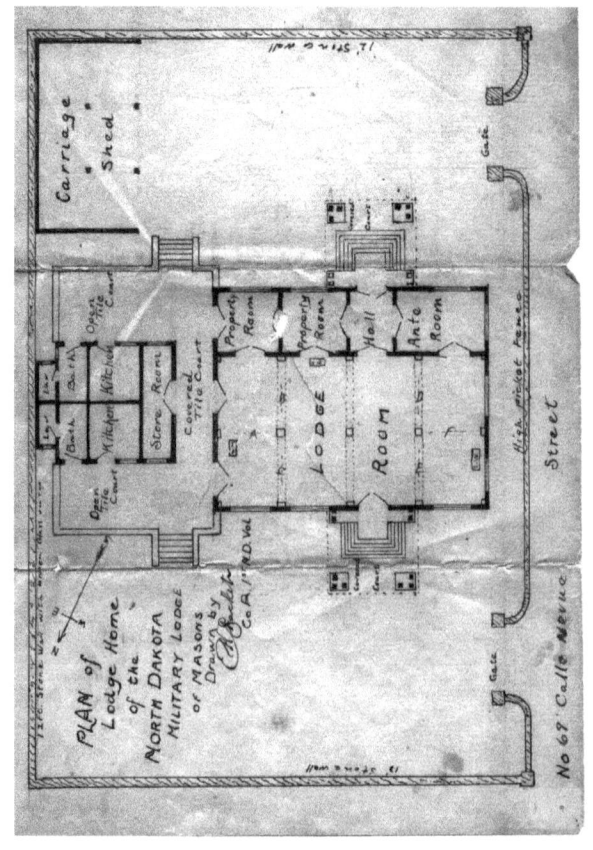

FIGURE 11: Floor Plan of North Dakota Military Lodge Home of Masons, Manila, P.I. Drawing by Eugene H. Sackett

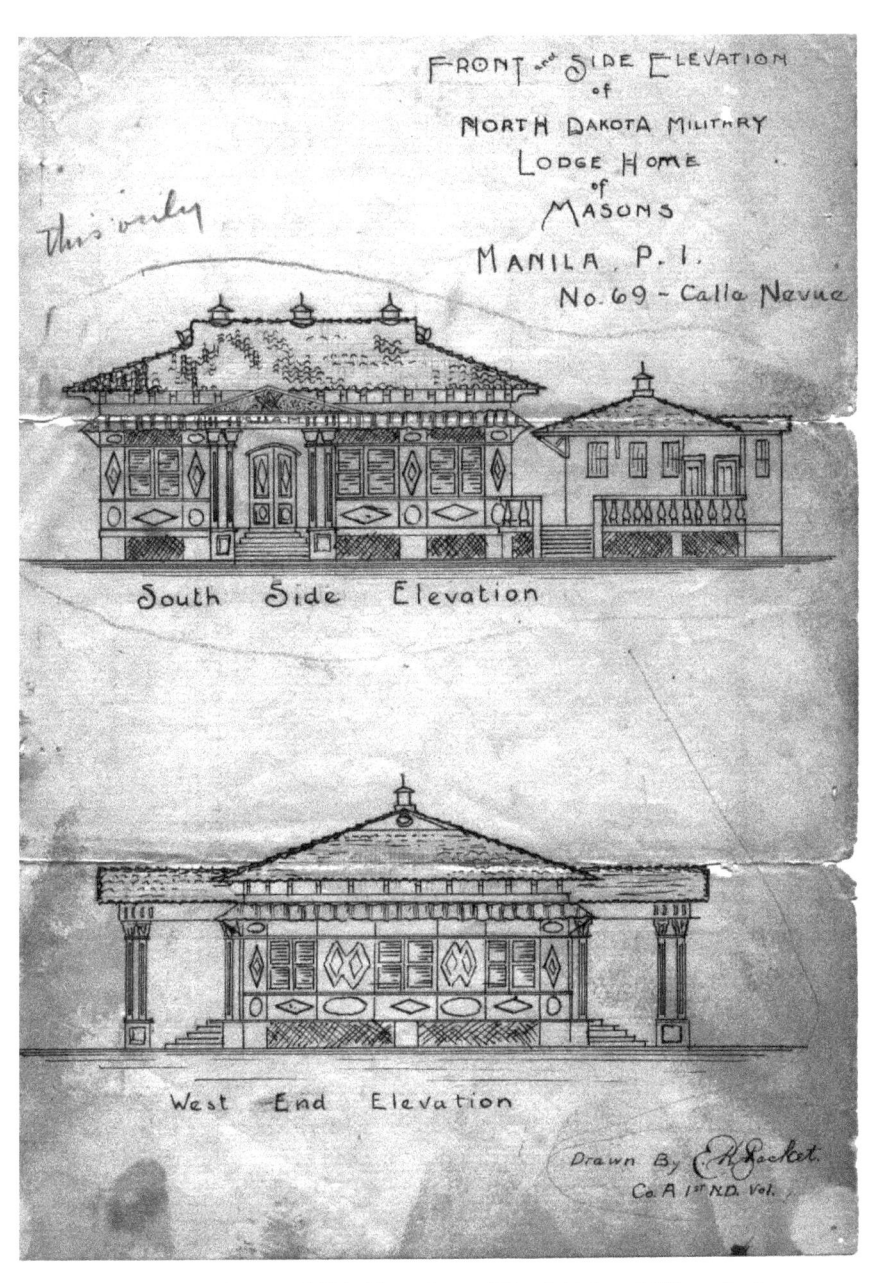

FIGURE 12: Front and Side Elevations of North Dakota Military Lodge Home of Masons, Manila, P.I. Drawing by Eugene H. Sackett

Many brother Masons from almost every state in the Union, from Isles of the Sea, from the far East and far West, have at various times visited the Lodge and participate in its meetings. A register of visitors was scrupulously kept, and is truly a Masonic curiosity, demonstrating beyond possibility of contradiction the universality of Free Masonary. Although it was not the intention of the original petitioners at the time of the inception of the idea to do much in the was of Esoteric work, a fast amount was done and much more f=refused, owing to lack of time. As it is, ninety-one applicants were initiated into the mysteries of the order, an twenty-three members of the other lodges affiliated. The outbreak o the insurrection put a sudden stop to the active work of the Lodge, and the regiment being now about to embark on its return to the United States, necessitate the closing of the firs American Masoni Lodge in the Philippines. Many of the craft, scattered throught the work, will, however, look back with the keenest pleasure to the Masoni Communion enjoyed at the Manila, through the North Dakota Military Lodge, Uniform Degree.

Camp Merrit, San Francisco
May 30, 1898 to June 27, 1898

May 30, 1898
Edgwood, California

Mr. J. Sackett
1430 5th Ave., S.
Fargo, N.D.

Dear Folks at Home:

We are on the Southern Pacific 9 miles from Mt. Shasta. It is a very grand sight. At every station we have been served to something - coffee-lunch-strawberries-roses-etc. Oregon beats them all for kindness. We stopped at Portland and were fed by the ladies of the Red Cross while the marine band played and the sailors of the Navy guarded us. I did not see John. Got into Tacoma Sunday 5 a.m. I am guard today and tonight. We get into San Francisco Tuesday morning.

E.H. Sacket

June 4, 1898

Dear Father and Mother:

It is 9:00 p.m. I am just going to bed and am alone so will write you a few lines.

The weather is beautiful here. Only a few drops of rain one night. Our camp is in very soft sand. This is very inconvenient. Today we went about 10 miles out to Golden Gate and saw the great large 16"-8"-12" guns. Also Dynamite guns. There were about 50' long. I should judge there were altogether 75 in sight and have been told there are 300 altogether. I feel as safe now in Frisco as I did in Fargo after seeing how well the harbor is protected. Our camp is about 5 miles out of the business center but there is 20 miles of street car beyond us. There are 14,000 soldiers.

We expect our clothing soon. We are given one suit of brown overall stuff to do fatigue duty in. You ought to see 1500 men come to order arms on the pavement with a crash as if one man had done it. Don't think N.D. do that for they sound like the purr of a clock when the pendulum is taken off.

Mrs. Latimer came to camp today and brought me cake-wash towels-rags bandages-soap for shaving face and clothing. All my tent mates said she could come as often as she wanted. She asked all about you and John's folks. I believe I told you that Uncle Eph, Aunt Hellen and Percy were to see Harvey and I. I am going to see both them and Mrs. Latimer. I bought a nice hand worked china silk handkerchief from a china man in china town for mother and will send it to you soon. It cost $1.50 but we got 4 at 20 cents each. Taps are sounding so I must close. Write Soon,

Your loving son, Gene

I am looking for something for Father.

Dear Mother:

I was over to Uncle Ep's last night and just got back this morning. This is Sunday June 5 and we have no drill. I picked this rose in their garden this morning. Their house is 4 miles from camp but it is over a high hill and to

get there by street car we have to go 15 miles, change five times all for 5 cents. I am going to church so good by. I got your letter yesterday. If you don't want the Zither give it to Miss Payne.
Gene

June 5, 1898
Camp Merrit
Frisco, Calif

Dear Mother:

I got a letter from you today stating you had received no letter or word from me. I can not see how this can be, as I have written every day to either you or father. I think the mail must have miscarried in some manner. I just received your letter of the 3rd to day so it only takes 5 days.

I spoke to Ed Gearey and he said that his wife complained of not receiving any letters from him. He thinks you are all impatient and so do I.

I was over to Uncle Eph's and also to Mrs. Latimer's. She gave me a towel and a pillow slip to put straw in. She is very comfortable situated and I had a pleasant time. Miss Hellen Carney is situated here doing stamping. I am going to see them some time.

I was on guard last night and yesterday. There is a thick fog and you can't see anything. Last night it was so thick you could not see an electric light half a block away. I was wet through and I took four hours today to clean my gun and clothes. Down town (5 miles) they do not get it so cold as they are back on the bay. But we can see the sun set in the water of the Pacific and the fog just rolls in on us. It is never very hot no matter how much sun there is.

We are very near to the Cliff House and Sutro Baths and we were out there day before yesterday for a bath. The view of the ocean and seals is fine. There is a park (finest I ever saw) hotel) Cliff House) ferris wheel (about 100 feet high) all kinds of 10 cent entertainments. The bath house has about five or six large baths as large as our lot all under cover. They are all at different temperatures so one can get any kind they want. I learned to swim. The salt water holds one up. Every thing is finished in marble and there are enough dressing rooms for 3,000 people.

FIGURE 13: Train to Sutro Baths. 51st Iowa camp on the left, Lone Mountain in the distance, and South Dakota Army on right. Summer 1898. From the Park Archives Collections, Golden Gate National Recreation Area, National Park Service, No. PAM Photo Prints, Box 3, F.62.

This noon I went down town with the bugler of our company. We met an old friend of his and he took us to the swellest restaurant in town. You bet I got one good meal. I bought me an aluminum plate, cup with cover holding 1 pint and a fork and spoon. Every thing in the store was made of aluminum, counters, doors, show cases, chairs, windows, etc.

I look for something for father but could find nothing useful. I was in the largest store in San Francisco. Show windows were two stories high. Large articles such as clocks, carpets, rugs, etc. were displayed on second floor. There was a telegraph station, post office, restaurant, barbershop and saloon in the store

FIGURE 14: Camp Merritt, Summer 1898. From the Photo Collections of Golden Gate National Recreation Area, National Park Service, No. GOGA-2418, Dan Reese-Camp Merritt Photo Collection.

June 9, 1898: I just got my brown suit this morning. I went to the Masonic Lodge with 35 others last night. The hall was the finest I have ever seen anywhere. Instead of woodwork of any kind, everything was mottled copper and was grand to look at. The degree work was fine.

Please write and tell me just when you get this letter and if you got the other things. Please write soon and plainer next time. Mr. Davis sends regards.

Gene

June 13, 1898
Camp Merrit
San Francisco

Dear Mother and Father:

I sent Father some papers with a Spaniard killer in them. Thought he would like it as a souvenir.

We got paid off Saturday and there were guards standing with 50 such shells in their belts.

It took about $25,000 to pay our reg. off. So you see there were quite a few gold cart wheels.

One of the boys lost his $20 piece in the soft sand and I went and got a plaster's sieve and we dug down all around in the tent about 18" before finding it, screening every shovel full.

I was over to Uncle Eph's Sunday. And met some very nice people. Brought home some roses.

I don't believe you would know me now with my duck suit, slouch hats, big shoes E-E, and tanned face. I keep my hair clipped short so I look too bad for the girls to get struck on me. I itch all over from fleas and my arm is quite sore from the vaccination.

The fog is a terror here when it is on and we have all colds. We have not straw to sleep on. They claim that straw spreads disease and so it had to go. It is damp and cold at night and warm in day time. I have been all over town and see some great sights. Stamford's house is made of stone that came around the Horn. You know he is relation to Stamford in Fargo. I don not like the common houses here, they are all made of wood.

We got paid Saturday and nest morning there were 25 men drunk and were not at roll call. The clerk was drunk and got fired and I was put in his place. So now I am Co. clerk and tent with 1st Serg't. We two are alone and it makes us plenty of room 10 x 12 tent. I do not have to drill or go on guard any more now and can go down town in afternoon.

FIGURE 15: Pay Day in the Army

I made a nice plat of the Co. street that can be used for showing where men stay as long as the company lasts. Everyone admires it.

June 15th: I have been very busy since moving in with 1st Sergeant and do not get much time to write. We put a board floor in tent yesterday so new we get little sand.

I went down town last night and got a fine bath at Y.M.C.A.

I found the paper of June 1st the day which tells of our coming to Frisco. I will send it to you. I subscribed for the *Examiner* (weekly) for Father.

Write soon,
Your loving Son
Gene

FIGURE 16: "Cease Firing!"—Co. F, 1st Colorado Infantry, U.S. Volunteers, Camp Merritt, San Francisco, CA.

June 17, 1898
Camp Merrit
San Francisco

Dear Mother and Father:

I wrote you day before yesterday but will write again. I have to stop now will commence again.

Saturday June 18: I was busy checking clothing, guns and everything and have little time to write. I have my new suit and look pretty good in it. I intend to have my picture taken tomorrow. I was over to Uncle Eph's last night just got back this morning. I do not know their number but they are on Diamond Street between 18th and 19th street, that will reach them.

My vaccinated arm is very sore. I cannot move it and it hurts me to cough or take a big breath. I have a very bad cold but can not cough.

Mrs. Latimer was over and brought me something to eat. She showed me the letter you wrote her.

I am glad you heard from Lyman. I will try and write to him.

Father will find a draft for $10.00 in this letter.

We are going to leave Frisco next Thursday on the *Valencia*. I am glad for if we stay here very much longer I will be busted.

Good by.
Gene

I expect I will not get an answer to this before I leave. I got your last letter with the one from Lyman in it June 16. I got 100 cards printed like the one in this letter.

George is working in Frisco. Willis is working I Wholesale House. Uncle is working at Navy Yard. Percy is selling papers. Mildred is taking music lessons. Alley is in Brooklyn, I think.

June 19, 1898
Camp Merrit

Dear Father:

I got your letter yesterday with the kisses and hugs for Ed Gearey. He appreciated them very much.

This has been a very windy rough day and I have been in bed. My tent came very near falling down.
I have felt badly all day, horrible pain in arm and head. I am only up now to finish this so you will get it tonight.

Uncle Epuram was over this morning and stayed till about 2:00 p.m. It made the time pass more easily. We talked of all the old Fargites we could think of.

He is working up a the Mare Island Navy Yard so this is the last time I will see him as it is about 35 miles up the bay from Frisco. He gets $3.75 a day and has to board himself off the island about three miles as they allow none to stay at yard at night except guards. He is looking well and sends his best regards to all. His address is 131 Diamond Street. I bought a pocket map of Frisco and will send it to you when we leave. I will mark on it where our camp is and where Uncle Eph lives. Also wharf where we landed.

That policy is a good thing I think as you explain it. So if you think best have it sent immediately as we leave very soon.

I hardly expect to get gone next Thursday as the Valencia is not repaired yet and that has to be done before we go on board. Use your own judgment about sending policy to me to sign.

I got a letter from Mr. Vance and for fear I do not get time to write to him please tell him all you can about me and give him my best regards. I wish he were along to jolly us up as most of us have never been to church. We have a C.E. tent to read and write in also a Y.M.C.A. tent.

One boy was buried yesterday and another today and still another was sent east. I understand there have been eight die since coming to Frisco. I have got exactly $10.00 and do not expect to need more.

Gene

June 19, 1898
Camp Merrit

Dear Mother:

I wrote to you yesterday and as this is Sunday I will write again.

Yesterday the Captain received orders to have his Company in readiness to go on board Valencia next Thursday. I think that is proof enough we are going. The Valencia is a very nice boat taking about 600 people.

We all have our new suits, hats, shoes, guns, belts, scabburds, leggins, overshirts, blue woolen undershirts (woolen), drawers woolen, socks woolen and cotton. I just gave in a new requisition for Co. A for all new goods. Each soldier gets two suits of thin cotton underwear to use over there. We also get white duck suits after we get on the boat. I ordered some woolen socks as my others are full of holes and I have nothing to mend them with.

I am sorry I can not get you anything more to remember Frisco by, but money is running short. If I can get away I am going down town and get my picture taken today.

We drill n Sunday now as well as other days so to be up to snuff by the time we go away. Today we practice shooting at targets. The 1st Sergt is very sick and I have to see to him. I am almost down myself but manage to keep a going. Dan Davis is in the hospital with his vaccinated arm. It is swollen from the wrist to the shoulder and is a bad sight.

I get all your bundles of papers and they are as good as food.

Last night I dreamed of home and thought I was there. It makes me kind of homesick this morning. Give my best regards to Aunt Azubah. I would like to see her.
I guess this is all for this time. I will try and write often before I go.

Good by,
Gene

June 23, 1898
Camp Merrit

Dear Father:

I got a picture of our camp and will send it to you telling all I can think of.

Field hospital in foreground-all these tents in this one square belong to this. When a person gets very sick they come here otherwise they are taken care of by the regimental hospital. N.D. regimental hospital is the three large tents and round one up at other end of our blck. On northwest corner of block is quartermaster's or commissary's tents where we get all supplies. You will notice N.D. soldiers on inspection at west side of camp in rod. Co. B is 1st row of tents on south end of N.D. Co. A is 2nd row of tents on south end of N.D. My tent (1st sergeant) is first in row. I marked it by small dot on tent in picture so you can tell. Every one says we have the nicest tent in camp. We have a regular table, floor, raised movable bed, shelves, and frame to fit tent over so we do not use ropes as they do not hold in soft sand. This is very nice as no matter how hard the wind blows our tent does not budge.

N.D. does not look so many here as when in Fargo but over in Iowa they 4,000 men quartered so you see there are quite a few men in this picture. The other camp covers three times the space that N.D., Mont., Iowa, and S.D. do.

Just south of our camp is Sutro Electric line which goes 3 miles to Cliff House and Sutra Baths west from camp or about 4 miles to town east. By town I mean water front. This is one of stylish parts of town where we are and it is a solid mass all around us.

Over soldiers heads (who are on inspection) may be seen the trees of the Presidio Drill Ground it is a large reserve of the Government, beautifully kept with great stone wall and iron gates fencing it off. It covers about 40 acres. Just north from S.D. camp you will notice a clump of buildings some of which are round. They all belong to a children's hospital and are free to all. I was over there and I never saw so many children before in my life.

You will notice wagon tracks in soft sand and also all the foot prints everywhere.

We were out target practicing yesterday and I went along behind the rest as my arm is too bad to drill with. I shot and made two straight bullseyes and then the sore in my arm burst as my gun kicked so and I rode home on the street car. I can not wear a coat on it now.

Tell Judge Pollock that I saw his brother here and was very pleased to find my name on Co. A marked by him as one of his (Judges) friends. He seems like a very nice man looks and acts very much like the Judge.

Now write and tell me when you get this. Mother does not tell me date of my letters which she receives.

Good by
Gene

Did you get letter with Well's Fargo draft for $10.00 in it? How much do I owe you know?

June 23, 1898
Camp Merrit

Dear Mother:

I received your letter Monday June 20. It was dated June 15. You spoke of receiving one from me on the 14th which I mailed the 9th. By the time you got this it will be quite a time let me know.

Glad Aunt is making rug for my room as I need it so just now. I wrote to her last night. I forgot to put in a handkerchief [sic] for her so will ask you to give it to her. Tell her that I am sorry I forgot it.

I have spent lots of money since coming here but do not need it when I get away and would like to have you folks have something to remember me and San Francisco by. Give my best love to Mrs. Eddy. Tell her I go and look in a certain persons watch over in "B" to see one of her daughters faces. It always does me good and is as good as chewing the other fellows gum till recess.

Tell her yes, my suit and hair is so near alike that Mr. Davis came very near shaving off coat instead of hair.

Tad has Kodak but I use it once in awhile. We do not cook ourselves but sill have Co. cook, he drunk half of time, so we get bad food some times. We eat in our own tents.

Yesterday Mrs. Latimer was over and brought a couple of other ladies. They brought 8 large grips full of nice pies, cake, biscuits, preserved fruit. We all ate dinner together and got picture taken. So if Tad gets them finished up before we go I will send you one. Do not worry about us starving to death.

Now I guess I will stop as I stole off from tent to write this.

Please write a little plainer and take all the paper you want for writing, do not write across ends. You may have to pay postage at that end before long as I am running out of stamp money.

I ordered a half dozen pictures, 1 for Jessie Payne, 1 for Jennie Condist, 1 to Mr. Vance, 3 to you folks. I would like to have Mr. Taylor have one if he has none and Aunt.

Good by
Gene

My pictures were taken at the "Elite" photograph studio, 838 Market St. Jones & Lotz, No. of plates 5425. If you have any trouble getting them write to this address r for new ones. I could not afford a dozen good ones so got 6. They will not be finished till I have gone but are guaranteed to be best made and delivered at their risk and expense-just for soldiers. They are the best photographers in the City. Mrs. R.A. Latimer, 3608 26th St., San Francisco.

June 24, 1898
Camp Merrit

Dear Mother:

I got your letter yesterday and will try and get an answer off to you today. I will try and write a little every day before we go.

You keep writing about us starving. Well I laugh and grow fat over it. You speak of 4 ft. tents. I have never seen any except dog tents or shelter tents.

One man lost his contract for delivering tainted meat to soldiers. So we get good meat now.

We got new tents large and nice 10 x 12 and only have from three to five men in each so that is not bad. The tents are not made as good as the old tents we had at Fargo so we still keep them. Those tents are the finest made in the world so do not believe the *Argus*.

We get all the bakers bread we can eat. Have pork in morning, fresh meat at dinner and supper (fine) and fish on Sunday. Milk gravy once a day, meat gravy or soup at every meal. Cold cabbage slow about twice each week also beans, prunes, or apricots, or peaches cooked as sauce every dinner. Now I tell you that is good enough for me. But I have three plates of my own so I do not mix prunes and milk gravy together as the other boys do. This makes everything taste better. Some of the boys always kick, kick, kick, so you can not blame them.

One hungerford in our company is always kicking about something, either his stiff neck, sore feet, lame knee, damp weather, hot weather, cold weather, small tent (10x12), long drill, sand, etc., etc., etc.

One day we just got off drill when the dinner call sounded and he kicked because he could not rest awhile before his meal. At night when we came in, supper was not ready for an hour. Then he said he did not see why they could not have supper ready when we got in.

I would rather drill then be clerk but my chances of being with 1st sergeant in state room on boat instead of down in dungeon with other. There are lots of advantages so I keep it. I will stop.

Write soon,
Gene

June 26, 1898
Camp Merrit

Mr. J.S. Sacket

I will write you a few lines today. This will be our last day on earth for a while I expect. Fifty of Co. "H" go today on another boat as there is no room for them on the *Valencia*.[7]

Clerk work is not hard but it keeps a fellow on tap all the time. Friday things let up a little and I got the afternoon off to go and see the Union Iron Works, where the *Valencia* was on dry dock.

The ship yard covers an enormous tract of land on the water front of the bay. Frank Anders of Co. "B" and myself took in things together and you

---

7   The Valencia was running between Seattle, Washington and Cordova, Alaska as part of the Gold Rush following the Klondike discoveries before being put into service to supply the Philippine Campaign.

know what I did not understand Frank told me. The yards are guarded and if we had not been dressed in the blue and good talkers we would not have gotten in. Once inside all was well-except our ears.

First we went all over the *Valencia*. She is a nice little boat but not much larger than the *Flyer* at Seattle. She was on dry dock which is capable of taking a very large ship up on. The Battle Ship *Oregon* has been on it.

On board the Valencia men were working as thick as rats putting in bunks, cold storage rooms, boilers, cooking stoves, mesh rows, etc. Each man gives $0.50 and is fed for the trip by the ship's cook.

The hurricane deck is arranged for about 100 officers. The main deck for 50. These are state rooms holding from three to nine, already built in the ship.

Dorm below are being arranged the bunks for the common soldiers. This deck is reached through the hatches and has portholes for ventilation. The bunks are \made of woven wire mattresses stretched on gas pipe frames, which swing up and down out of way when not in sue. In front to keep from rolling out is a guard iron. Each man has a single berth or bunk. They are arranged three deep.

The chief engineer told me he was ordered to have steam on Monday.

The next thing I saw was the Jap cruiser which is very nearly ready to be launched. She has the most graceful lines of any ship I ever saw. Her great quadruple engines are one great mass of beauty, grace, and strength. They were tested, and run while I was there. It was a sight for your life. Four Jap inspectors stood by watching with eyes like serpents, yet as pleased as children.

Camp Merrit, San Francisco   45

Next in the yard was a U.S. torpedo boat about like the one we saw at Seattle, but she is not near completed yet.

The Battle Ship *Wisconsin* comes next. She is the largest the U.S. has ever started and is just one great floating fort. She will not be finished yet for two years. Everything is made f steel and painted red to keep from rusting. At every point in the yard nearly were blue prints showing some part of her upon which workmen were laboring. There were plenty of other boats building but I did not look them over.

Next I took in the buildings. First the great building where they bring parts of the great engines to be put together. Here are the parts of the engines for the *Wisconsin*, all laying around everywhere. That was the first job I ever saw where I did not want to tackle it and put things together. Next I went into the machine shop and saw all kinds of machinery. I could think of some I couldn't think of and some I can't yet think of. This building was larger than all the N.P. Shops at Fargo taken together. I wish Archie Cone could be there and run short on expressions.

The next place I went into was the pattern shop and I would like to work there, everything is so exact. Next and last but not least I went into the iron foundry. They were preparing to cast the base f one of the turrets for the Battle Ship *Wisconsin*. It was a grand sight to see a man turn a little handle on a rheostat up on the great electric crane and take 25 tons of melted iron across the great room and pour it into the great mold. Never a hand touched the ladle to steer it. All done by a man from above. This was the last and I came away.

In the evening 18 of us went over to Oakland to lodge. Some gentlemen had been out and invited us. Unfortunately we had not found just where to go so through instruction of a policeman who said he was also invited we walked about a mile over to an electric line and got back to Oakland at about 10:00 p.m. Having gone 37 miles out of our road for 5 cents. We saw part of the lodge work however and then repaired to the banquet hall to one of the finest I have ever been seated to.

We then recrossed the bay on the ferry and as we got back to Frisco noticed a fire and went to it. It was a blister. There were seven fire engines just working for all they were worth, throwing water and two chemical engines throwing chemicals on the fire. The buildings were all shacks but were soon under control and we started for home only to find the street car stopped and we had to walk about 2 miles home.

My guitar is all right and is right in tent and have a concert quite often. Keeps me alive till I come back.

Here is the cost of our clothing. This is exact from Government Official Price List as I have it and have to charge each man.

Woolen Blanket	2.83
Blue Blouse	3.25
Canvas Coat	1.04
Drawers	.40
Campaign Hat	.84
Flannel Overshirt	1.94
Undershirt	.38
Shoes	.89
Stockings (cotton)	.06
Stockings (wool)	.23
Canvas Leggins	.55
Canvas Trousers	.94
Kersy	2.32

Keep sending letters as they will be forwarded, address to Camp Merrit till I write you different.

Gene

June 27, 1898
Camp Merrit

Dear Mother:

We are breaking camp now to go to boats. We leave at 11:00 a.m.

You write me just the same and it will be forwarded. God by till I hear from you again.

Gene

Figure 17: Leaving the Presidio, San Francisco, to embark for Manila

FIGURE 18: Transport "Pennsylvania" leaving San Francisco with Thirteen Hundred Volunteers for Manila

FIGURE 19: U.S. Troops leaving San Francisco for Manila

FIGURE 20: A Thousand Boys in Blue on S.S. Rio-de Janeiro bound for Manila.

Transport to Manila, Philippine Islands
June 28, 1898 to July 24, 1898

June 28, 1898
Aboard *Valencia*

Dear Father:

This is probably the last I will see of the U.S. for awhile.

It is 4:00 o'clock p.m. and we are casting off and pulling out into Pacific Ocean.

Write to me and I will get it at Honolulu.

Good by,
Gene

July 3, 1898
Str. Valencia

Dear Folks at Home:

Left Frisco, Tuesday June 25 at 4:30 p.m. I mailed a postal to father at that time. I want you to tell me when you get this letter and give me date it was written (July 3). I wish to know how long it takes to go to Fargo.

We left Frisco next day after the main fleet left as we were not ready to go with them. We backed out from the dock which was fairly alive with waiving white handkerchiefs of pretty California girls. As we steamed down the water front every whistle (hundreds) blew great long and short blasts of farewell and God speed. At 5:00 p.m. we steamed through Golden Gate past the great frowning guns and were there signaled a last farewell by the signal corpse f the soldiers at the Presidio. Directly the vessel felt the heaving of the great ocean and so did every lad on her. Before we were out of sight of the Cliff House I had that awful feeling and adjourned below to a more favorable position of bunk as did many others.

The wind was fresh, the sea high and the boat gave no rest to the weary.

Excuse me for using both sides of the paper but I can not tell when I will get more. I slept below the first night and it was bad. Every one was of the same opinion that there was something in the stomach which they did not like, so we all spit it out and very soon the place looked sick. To add to the fun the goat gave an ugly roll and shipped a great quantity of salt water. It came down the hatches and drowned out the boys who were sleeping near the hatch and on the lower tier. For two days there was about 6" of water swishing across the floor from one side to the other with caps, knapsacks, coats, leggings, shoes, guns, haversacks, cups, pens, bayonets and every thing that belongs to a soldier floating around in it. I took good precautions however and when we first went into the boat and hooked every thing else to it so the boat could roll all she wanted to without dislodging them. Then I was ready for anything that came. And my gun did not get a speck of rust on it.

I lay in bed all the next day till 11:30 p.m. without food (I had no use for it) and then summoned courage to go on deck. After this I only threw up once and so did not go below again for I knew the fowl air would make me sick again.

July 5: Thursday morning I went below to get some sleep. I had been asleep about 2 hrs when they decided to clean things up. Well the corporal who woke me up shook me by my left arm tearing the vaccination all to pieces. You bet I was awake. The arm is a sight to see, broke out all over and is very very sore. I have it dressed every day and sometimes twice. I get very little sleep with the swelling and pain from it. The doctor said I should not be below so I have a bunk in a state room with Gods sunlight and air coming through two portholes. The doctor says I may be laid up for two months, but I don't believe it. But I am going to take care of myself. The sore is as large as this circle [one inch diameter circle drawn] and day before yesterday it was as large as a good sized marble. It has made me sick a bed ever since. So I did not celebrate the 4th. Hidreth howled, and they made other speeches and kept a small canon going all day.

The officers had three swell meals, and the common herd went to their pork, hardtack and coffee with no sweetening. It is a shame how they feed us. Frisco was a paradise besides this. We do not live half as well as the meanest convict in any state prison in America.

The meat instead of being cooked is steamed and fried up till it is unfit for a dog. I do not receive any soft bread as the steamship company contracted for, but get hardtack. I get water instead of coffee and eat plain hardtack and water, as I can not go the meat. The hole of the ship has got lots of tomatoes, canned corn, canned corn beef, etc. but we get none of it, and it is my opinion they intend to sell it at Honolulu. We got the officers to kick once and next meal was better but it is same now. Every one is strapped so we can not buy anything. But it would take a fortune to get anything, 15 cents for a small cup of coffee.

We are about 200 miles from Honolulu now and expect to get there tomorrow before the other fleet gets in as we go faster.

I talked an arm off the 1st engineer and we are bosom friends now. He is going to help me and I will draw a diagram of the boat and send it to you to let you see where I am, etc. I do {?} to get this done however before we get to Manila, so be patient.

I spend a great deal of time in the engine room as it just suits me and then there are not 600 running against my arm. Doctor says it is good as it keeps me warm and sets the filth out of my body.

The engines are very good ones and I am learning a good deal. There are shore baths and one tin bath on the boat, so we all keep clean. Every one is required to keep clean and is put in guard house if found dirty. They throw the ticks overboard so to avoid disease. The boys don't kick as the wire mattresses are very easy. No ticks above were thrown overboard as the beds have slats.

I will stop for this afternoon, may put in more before I get to Honolulu. However I hope this is enough for once. You can let the people at home read this and please save all my letters so I can see them when I come home.

Give Mrs. Laizure and Bill also the kids my best regards. Tell Clyde if he thinks we are out on a pleasure trip he is d - - d badly mistaken, but I would not go back for a good deal now as every day I learn, see, and hear things I never dreamed of and can only be gotten on a trip of this kind. For one thing the Cap. Of the ship taught me how to get longitude, latitude and time from the sun with the sextant.

Wednesday July 6: We are nearing land today and expect to see it about 4 p.m. Land birds are seen now flying about.

The doctor dressed my arm himself and says "pretty sore arm." It is draining pretty hard now so I think it is going to be better soon. There is a ridge under my arm at the shoulder as large and long as my two fingers. My chest is sore so I can not cough or take a big breath.

2 p.m. Very finest shoreline about 150 miles away. Sea has so far been quite smooth but now beginning to grow choppy.

6 p.m. Mountain very plain lower land not in sight yet. The clouds hang round top and in few places can see snow (in torrid zone). I have a notion to put on a pair of rubber boots and walk over and bring back some to cool water which is not fit to drink. Water is god but warm. There is a volcano on the mountain and a faint film of smoke can be made out. Numerous islands are in sight now. Very indistinctly can be seen the island with Honolulu on it.

11 p.m. I was awakened by hand, went n board and found we were in harbor with 13,000 other soldiers and 6 gun boats. Bells rent the air and whistles blew themselves hoarse.

The band on a tug and played every one of the national airs. I sat there in the dark with the tears just streaming down over my cheeks it sounded so god and I felt so good.

July 7 at Y.M.C.A. building: this morning the Newport came in with two very important thins on board. 1st - Gen. Merritt, 2nd - Mail. Think more of last and hope I will get letter from you.

I started up town and it was pretty hard navigating as my arm hurt from stepping and my head light. I had just about decided to return when three ladies in a double carriage beckoned me to ride with them. They are from Ohio, Michigan, and Mass respectively and were normal teachers in a girls' boarding seminary. They took me all over town and it is simply grand to see the trees, coconuts, pineapples, bananas, etc. I saw the palace of Queen Lill, Government Buildings, etc. There is a free school system and English is taught throughout the republic. So you would not know you were out of the U.S. except color.

Now I will quite as I have to get back tot he boat to go to a grand dinner given to the soldier boys under the spreading trees of one of the parks. I saw the tables and don't want to miss it. This is the finest city I have ever seen. Now good by. Address to:

Transport ship *Valencia*
Bound for Manila
Gene

The Legislature of Honolulu passed resolutions to let all soldiers letters go free of charge. I sent you a map of Frisco to let you know where we were. Also receipt for photographs which I had taken and were to be sent (3) to you. If you want more send receipt to them and you can get same as I could not afford more. I have big sum of 70 cents.

FIGURE 21: Executive Palace, Honolulu, Hawaiian Island. Strohmeyer & Wyman Publishers, N.Y.

We got in last night at 11:00 p.m. I am very sick and will ask you to go and read Mothers letter which will tell of my trip up to 11:30 a.m. today. I have been on the go most all day and now it is very painful to write but could not skip you. Let my folks read this so as to get full detail of stay here.

I went out of "G" at 11:30 and another kind lady gave me ride to boat. I got permission to start alone for lunch grounds. I got stick for cane and took five rests on the way which was about ¼ mile. When I got there (this was the grounds around the capital building) this finest foliage I ever saw. I was very near up a stump. But another kind lady told me to get into the back seat of her carriage. It was a [?] carriage which probably cost from $600 to [?]. I felt mean in there but forgot my troubles to {?}{?} was a sleeping beauty for I don't know how long as they would not tell me. I was awakened by the band of the escort followed by the 6,000 hungry boys. Our regt. Did not come until 1:30 and in meantime the gentleman who owned the rig made his appearance: He was a Senator and very rich. Then I did feel small, but he began and I never saw a nicer man. He went and got a big tray of dinner and a box, put the box on the seat, put the tray on the box then commenced talking. He was from Ohio. That diner-fine coffee, cold water, delicate sweet bread and butter, cheese, small onions, pineapples, oranges, bananas, etc. and oh? Two kinds of pie. I commended before N.D. had come in the gate and finished after they did. Then I went up to their house which was very grand. Then they drove me most f the afternoon. The rubber tire of wheels made one think I was in paradise. All this drive was taken by me with his lovely daughter alone except for little Ethel (you had better look out). She is a fine Christian girl belongs to the Congregational Church. We returned for afternoon lunch. I was then invited by the Senator to stay all night. I had to report, however at 6:00 p.m. and so the grand lady went with me to get-Colonel (no little Capt consent in this affair) consent. But he could not let me go as he was just ordered to report at head quarters and he did not want anyone off until he knew orders. So I am in old bunk tonight. Orders are to go at 7:00 n

the morning. We are all kept on. The young lady gave her my card and address and I think she may write to Mother. I will quit.
Gene.

July 24, 1898
On Board *S.S. Valencia*

Dear Ones at Home:

We passed the Madrone Islands last night, and expect to see northern part of Philippine Islands next Wednesday morning. We were in sight of land all yesterday afternoon. It was a regular large smoking volcano. The smoke just poured out and at night it was all red with fire. You better believe it was a sight. This was the first sight of any account since leaving Honolulu July 9.

We crossed over the 180th meridian at 6 p.m. Thursday therefore for the rest of that day it was Friday. Peculiar as it may seem when it is 1:00 a.m. Sunday morning here it is 11:00 p.m. Friday evening at Fargo (about the time mother goes into her tantrums about doors back and front).

We are getting short on water so that coffee is made of condensed sea water. The meat is not good on account of heat. I have no kick coming on food as I have been in hospital ever since we left Honolulu. We get tea and toast (that is all we are supposed to get) but once in a while oatmeal with brown sugar is served and once in a while soup and also canned peaches. Clambroth one and canned salmon. Jelly on toast. We are never allowed fresh meat.

When we left Honolulu Doctor Pease ordered me into hospital and I have been there ever since and liable to be for some time. I have not been able to sit up and for about 8 days have not been allowed to move out of bed or roll over. An abscess formed under my arm in pit of shoulder as large as an orange. The doctor lanced it and a stream of puss as large as a pencil ran out. This relieved me as I had not slept for three nights. That morning the bandages had to be removed five times to allow puss to run out. As it runs out under bandage it destroyed skin. This produced a burning sensation the worst I ever had. They probed the abscess and the ball of the probe came away through the arm and showed under the skin on the upper side. When the pus got so it did not run much the blood began to run. At this the doctor placed me on my back and would not let me up for anything. They fed me with a spoon and gave me a lot of medicine to stop blood flowing and strengthen walls of arteries. Since I got over the worst the doctor told me if the artery in my shoulder (which had been undermined by abscess) had bursted as he expected it would they would have had to cut my arm off. It is better now.

July 31: Have been discharged from hospital, every one is as we are entering Manila Harbor. We are the only boat that has not buried some one at sea. We got out of water yesterday so left other boats behind as we are faster and are getting to Manila as quick as possible. It rained all day and night so we will not go thirsty.

After leaving Honolulu I read over all the letters I received from you and will answer some questions which I did not before on account of bustle of camp.

Father asked about guitar. I have it in hospital with me and play every day. It helps to pass away the time and they all like to hear it. It is carried as A Com. Property.

Father may give a good big piece of cake to Fig for me.

Kodak - Tad Foster had it along with us.

The pictures of my western trip I gave to Albrant and never got any more. If you can find negatives upstairs (they are all in a roll) you can get some finished up. I promised John some and wish you could send him some. Go to Judd with negatives and he will fix as many as you want. I will settle with you.

I got all papers you sent me.
Use pillow to put all my socks, etc. in.

Harvey has been sea sick nearly all the time on the trip. He is homesick and I can see is sick of the job but does not say anything about it.

Give my best regards to Lyman, John, Mrs. Walters, Mrs. Eddy, Mr. Vance Taylor, Amerland, Frank Thompson, Friedlander, Judge Pollock, Frank Knerr, Tom Barlow and all the Y.M.C.A. boys. Also tell Aunt I think about that rug every morning when I get up.

Aug. 1: It rained so hard last night that they could not stay near land and ran by the harbor by mistake. This morning they put back and got to harbor just as other boats came up, we are all entering harbor now. Can see town. It is raining harder then ever saw it in N.D.

Got into anchorage at Cavete about 12:45 p.m. there are war vessels and transports and coaling vessels all sides of us. The masts and smoke stacks of the wrecked and sunken Spanish vessels are sticking up right near us and in many places are red flags indicating wreckage under water. We have heard no news yet so you people know more about what is occurring here then we do. We will be landed today we all expect but may be kept on board for a week as they are preparing places for us.

Across the bay 10 miles may be seen the glistening of the sun on the buildings of the city of Manila and off to the left in the harbor are the many vessels of foreign nations. The English and German are great, floating forts, the

English are white. This is a grand big harbor. They say it is the largest in the world and all the Navies in the world could maneuver in it at once. It is so wide can not see across.

Just got news from a correspondent who was on board representing the "London Times" that Sampson had destroyed Spanish fleet and Hawaii had been annexed. Manila is being besieged by the Astor Batter who are entrenched three miles out. We heard firing last night and probably it was them.

As soon as the boats got in Natives came along side in small boats full of fruit of all kinds, but the surgeon general prohibited the soldiers from buying any. This is a good thing for the boys who have money as they won't get sick and good for us poor fellows who haven't money and would have to stand by with the water running out of our mouths.

We have to get our mail off tonight as a ship starts with mail for the U.S. tomorrow so I may not get any more in this letter so, Good By

Gene

P.S. How do you like the letters? Are they too long?

FIGURE 22: Wreckage of Spanish Ship, Manila Bay, Philippine Islands.

Letters From Manila— Camp Inartel de Malatee
August 19, 1898 to January 1, 1899

August 19, 1898
Manila, Philippines

Dear Ones at Home:

Got letters from Father, Mother, Blanche, Mrs. Matson of Minneapolis (my traveling friend from Seattle). All got here Aug. 7 (for my Birthday), papers of all kinds. Father's is dated June 25, Mother's is dated June 25-26-29–July 1, Aunts is dated June 25.

I will say that I have not been homesick as mother says of J. Geary although would like to see you all. I wish all of you would not worry about us so, there is no need of it.

The boys went off boat at Caveitee last Sunday week and I was left on, on account of arm which does not need any care now.

Last Friday the bombardment of Manila commenced at 10:00 a.m. and lasted 2 hrs. total success for Americans. One of the N.D. boys was shot through ankle in battle and since one has been killed accidentally by another loading gun Co. C. They are camped in a rice slew and are out or short of food so I am fortunate in being here although if I could I would be there. Sunday we left Cavite and anchored in front of Manila and are now discharging cargo. Will be through tomorrow and will then go ashore.

May not write so often then, but will try and write once a week but do not worry for steamers going home are few and far between.

There are great war vessels and other ships on all sides of me now and I don't think any more of them than I did the hills of potatoes in our back yard. I can say that I have smelled gun powder you bet the Old *Olympia*'s guns make a noise when they salute. They are saluting someone all the time so we don't pay much attention to it all. I keep on reading. Just heard that peace had been declared Aug. 12, don't know how true it is but hope so. There are 6,000 Spanish prisoner soldiers here feeding on our flour and I want it stopped. Manila is a fine town for a Spanish town, has electric lights and street cars, pavement and 450,000 people, but no docks so that boats have to be brought alongside of ship which makes slow work with 300 tons freight.

FIGURE 23: Envelop from Eugene Sackett with drawing of ships in Manila Bay.

I saw the finest sunrise this morning of all my life. It rose over a great mountain and the waters of the bay were so still that you could see masts in water.

This is all for this time. Send stamps but not many at time. Good by till I write again. Hope to see you soon.

August 26, 1898
Manila, Philippines

Dear Father and Mother:

Received your letters of July 5-12-18 and will write you to let you know I am on shore again after a stay of 55 days on shipboard.

All the provisions are off the *Valencia* and she has started back to the U.S. I think. She has a splendid of gentlemanly officers and I was sorry to leave them. They treated us six boys who stayed after the crowd was gone very nicely.

We were landed in a small steam launch and saw the wrecks of the Spanish boats sunken in the mouth of the river upon the day of the battle July 13 to keep the *Monteray* from getting too near to the city.

The N.D. troops are quartered in the Native soldiers quarters which are made of bamboo and straw built about 4 feet from ground each building measuring 25 x 100 or thereabouts. Two companies are quartered in each building. They are on the sea beach which makes the air fresh, bathing pleasant.

There are soldiers barracks or hospitals all over town and everything that belongs to the government has the Spanish Crown on it. Catholic churches are very numerous with their moss covered exteriors and dark interiors.

This has been a grand town some day but between earthquakes and lack of Spanish money to keep it up nearly everything has fallen into decay. All the nice places are mostly owned by foreigners. These are models of excellence and it is a pleasure to the eye but all around them sprinkled in like salt are the huts of the poorer then poor Natives. This spoils the scene for me.

FIGURE 24: United States Monitor "Monterey"

The old town is entirely surrounded by a wall eight feet think bristling with old brass cannon green with age.

Most of the new buildings are made of wood for evidently the people paid dearly for their experience with the old stone structures. Everywhere may be seen the ruins of old stone buildings shook to their foundations by earthquakes.

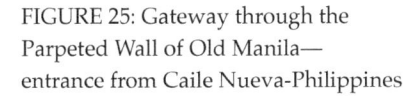

FIGURE 25: Gateway through the Parpeted Wall of Old Manila—entrance from Caile Nueva-Philippines

Frank Anders is some what on the sick list and most of the other boys also from bad water, bad mutton, and hot weather. We are all black and dirty. Every one needs a shave.

Got two bundles of papers, one with my letter in it. I don't think I care for you to print my letters as I am out of practice and don't like to see them in print.

I guess I will stop now till I have got something to say, good by.

Gene

FIGURE 26: Old Spanish Battery—Luneta, Manila

FIGURE 27: Modern Spanish Battery on Luneta, Manila.

FIGURE 28: Looking Northwest from Tower of the Church of Ronondo, Manila, Philippine Islands.

Harvey is well and as he does not hear from home as often as I do I let him read your letters and I read his. He spoke about insurance said it would be too bad to loose it but guessed I didn't look as though I would give you a chance to loose it so don't worry anymore.

I did not get John's letter of introduction. I would write him but have forgotten his address. It keeps all my spare time occupied to write you.

Hope I get paid soon so I can send some home to help out while Father is sick.

I am making a map of the battle of July 13 but it is slow work. Will send it home as soon as I find out whether you received the one of S. Frisco.

I can't write much at a time as there is too much noise.

Mother has written me so far 29 letters all of which I have yet.

FIGURE 29: Rosario Street and Binondo Church, from the Pasiq River, Manila, Philippine Islands.

FIGURE 30: Escolta, the principal business street in Manila, Philippine Islands.

FIGURE 31: The Beautiful Church of San Sebastian-built of steel, Manila, Philippine Islands.

September 10, 1898
Manila, Philippines

Dear Mother:

Your letter of July 22 reached here Sept 4 and the one of July 26 reached here today. I was glad to receive both. Sorry your foot got hurt. Will say I am getting along all right, work and eat as hard as anyone else now, my arm is almost healed over now and only bothers a little so you see I need no sympathy from you now and don't want you to worry so. You ought to be glad to be alone for awhile. Was glad to get money. Everyone laughed when they saw how the money was sowed into your letter to one. I did not get any letters from you while at Honolulu. The only one I got there was Mr. Lajures. You speak of stamps in letter from Honolulu. I want you to save them for that Government paid for all that. Your letters have postage due marked on them but I have never been asked for it.

Everyone was very kind about coming into hospital while I was sick to see me. We have some fine officers. I gave up the clerkship and am not sorry. There is too much books to keep here where man are loosing things every day and new has to be provided. We do not get full rations now and it has to be figured up equally between each man by clerk.

John Geary is getting fat and has quite a growth of whiskers. I weigh about 160 now. I sent or had sent photograph and papers from [?] office for Mrs. Lajure also. I forgot to return John's letter and will try and think to put it in this time.

I am now looking at your letter of July 26. I always hold you in my hand when I write. Glad you got letters and photos and glad the photos were good. As I remember Jennie Condit has one, Miss Payne has one, Mr. Vance and Mr. Taylor has one, and you have two.

I thought you knew what a sextant was. It is used to find time and position no the ocean from the sun or stars. The heavens are only suited near the horizon only needing 1/6 of a circle for measuring the degrees on. Hence the name of the measuring instrument Sextant.

It seems funny to me of you speaking of a green yard and new peas and corn, etc. By the time your letter reached me the grass begins to fade and peas, corn are of the past. I have wondered if grass has been hoed out of ditch in front this year. I hope Mr. Morris is better. Ed Geary prizes very highly the picture I took of his children. He has one taken by Judd but thinks mine is the best. Ed is liked by all the boys in the regiment. I always call him just plain Ed. I can't get used to Lieutenant.

I was surprised to hear of Florence getting married. I always thought Luella would first.

I am sorry to hear of Hail in N.D. The war ought to bring a good price on wheat and every farmer ought to have lots of money to stand the tax.

I wish I knew the address of that photograph company in Frisco, I would give them the best glowing up I could for their unbusiness like manner. I wish you would drop them a letter. I was out of paper and got this in Manila. It will not stand pen and so I have to write with pencil. Hope it will stand till it gets home. We will have a great time reading all the letters over again when I get home. I have received about 34 from you. How many have your received from me? I received a letter from Mrs. Lajure today.

Today we had regimental inspection of arms and had to stand out in the sun at attention for over an hour not being permitted to raise our hand to wipe the swet from our face. As a result 4 in our company were taken in from sunstroke. The sergeant put a stop to the monkey work and says if they want to inspect, do it by moonlight.

At about 10:30 a great commotion was raised by 4 Spaniards (prisoners held by Agiwolda) running into camp. We were all called out in a hurry and B and G are out at front nights on account of Natives who are mad because of General Merrit not allowing them to rob the town. I think we are liable to have serious trouble yet and I hope so for I wasn't there last time. These 4 Spanish soldiers say that there are still a lot more of prisoners too weak to get away.

I could keep on writing for a week about things I see here, but you must be tired.

Blanch Sawyer acts like a fool in writing to me. She seems to think she must have a letter every time you do. I don't think I will write to her as often as I have. Her letters are as soft as puddin.

Give my best regards to all.
Gene

September [?], 1898
Manila, Philippines

Dear Mother:

I was glad to receive letter from you. You always have something interesting to say. I am sorry you were sick and hope you are better by this time. Would have liked to have been home and had some peas and corn out of the garden. All the vegetables we get here are evaporated like I saw at Seattle for Klondikers. They are not as good as the real articles.

Wish I was there to bother you with drawings for McCormick. I suppose Friedlander has plenty of work but not much else for me. I would like to take a look at the new depot and several other buildings spoken of in their speech.

I hope the paving will not make your taxes higher but if it comes to the corner you must learn to ride my wheel to and from work. You will have plenty of space for head way room.

I would like to have my wheel here now, a lot of the boys brought their wheels over and now go around sailing while we look on and grin.

We have had two Masonic meetings here and two candidates. More on way. I am glad I am one of them. It gives me something to study about. So far as I know this is the only lodge in the Philippines.

I am getting used to laying around now so am not so impatient to be going home as I was but I would like to be there just the same. I am doing full duty now and work all I can for I feel better when I do. All work is done in cool part of day. Last night trouble was expected from the Natives. So we all had to sleep with all clothes on, our gun by our side. Harry Berry - Chief Trumpeter - asks for you every time I hear from Home. He says the Stilwells never write anymore. I have a map of the town now out of a book and will try to draw a map of the battlefield and send it to you. Thanks for the $2.00. I will pay it back. Want a statement of account from you please. Will write soon again.

Gene

September 18, 1898
Iuartel de Malate
Philippines

Dear Father and Mother:

No mail has come in since receiving your last letter, but have some spare time, will write you a few lines. We are all looking for newspapers with account of battle of Aug 13. They ought to be on next mail. I am feeling tip top, having lots of fun and just as soon stay as long as we get used this way. However, I go pretty light on water. It and meat and beans have bad effect.

The ladies of Bismark sent the Co. about $60.00 as a Co. fund. This helps to fill up low places in grub pile. We get rice, oatmeal or prunes once a day. this makes us lick our chops. Twice a week we get pancakes with syrup.

Co. B has moved from barracks to quarters about a mile south of us near the fort. So we have the room to ourselves now and are all inside instead of in tents and under house. Beds will be issued to us in a few days. These are of iron with can seat bottoms. One for each man. Co. G has also gone out about ½ mile east of Co. B leaving Co. H one room. This makes it so I seldom see Harvey now but he is down to Headquarters every evening so I see him once a day.

I am located in one corner of room so I get plenty of light and fresh air. Both needed. I bunk with a slow easy good old man named Tom Peterson. He is all right for me though.

Next to us is Sergt. Louden and Sergt. Sperry. Both are fine boys, full of fun and very good and kind friends to me. Both have their applications in to join the Masons here. This will make four in Co. A. My chief occupation now-days is drawing and rounding up live stock. However as the majority of the boys have no hand for the first, I have none for the last. They do not seem to like me very much and get off me as soon as possible. I spend about 6 hrs a day drawing except those days I have something else to do. Will send you a sunset view which I drew. Every one wants me to make one for them but I don't think. You can judge for yourselves as to its worth. It is done on very poor paper but all I could get.

Yesterday I had lots of fun. I was placed on wood detail and we had to wade out to some old thatch houses which were built out over surf on piles. I waded in with clothes on. Water was warmer than air. It was about ¼ mile out to huts. The beach is very gradual here. You can go out ½ mile before having to swim (in some places). The sea was running pretty brisk and went over my head every time. I have got used to it by former experience. Once out to the house, the fun began. The piles were slippery and we had some backsliding before reaching line of floor. However when we did reach it, axes soon made havoc of wood work. The wood was tumbled into sea and tide setting in floated it shore.

When we tried to get back to shore found tide had raised quite a bit so we had to swim for a way. Among other things taken by Uncle Sam were shoes for Spanish soldiers, 150,000 pairs. These are given to the American soldiers free gratis for nothing, and come in handy as most of us needed shoes. They are high tan and we can put bottom of pant legs inside.

We all have white suits now for dress and it looks very nice to see N.D., Idaho, Minn., and 14 regulars come out on the street and form on dress parade or retreat roll call while the stars and stripes are being run down for the night.

I think, though, if the people there could get a sight of us when in our brown suits ready for outpost duty with our battered tin plate and cup tied to us and a ragged blanket around our shoulders they would not think us quite so neat. Especially if they could see us lie down on a hard floor or stone walk after being relieved from outpost duty and be sound asleep in two shakes of a lambs tail, I think they would say our minds were free and we were in good health. So we are most of us.

All the insurgent forces (about 5,000) have marched out of the City leaving us entire possession. I was on duty when they passed and stood at present arms while passing. The leaders of their companies and regiments seemed tickled to see me. Our Lieutenant said that was right a little molasses in the right place suited the flies. This makes duty a little easier for us now as not so many outposts are needed. As long as they were in town the Natives and Spaniards assumed we could not do the thing alone. But have changed their mind now I guess.

The paymasters are paying off the troops now as fast as possible and we hope by Monday to get our cart wheels.

The Y.M.C.A. has started up here as you see by my letter heading. It is a fine thing for the boys. Writing material is furnished and also some reading matter. They have meetings Sundays and Wednesday eve. Two B & H burners hanging lamps are kept burning every night till after taps. They are located in a nice building having two large rooms. It is right in midst of camp.

We hear all kinds of rumors about going home but nothing very officious. However, Harvey told me that we would not be here long and would be home for Xmas so prepare for me. I told Chas. Furrel in a letter to him that I would eat Xmas turkey with him this year.

I have read in the *"Youth's Companion"*, often about people talking about what they would eat when they got back from a place where they could not get it and I used to laugh to think how foolish they were. But now see how it was. We are doing the same thing. One will say - "Wish I had some strawberries.

Then another - "Would not want them without some sugar & cream"

No. one will say - "Oh! You are too particular, cream without strawberries or sugar would satisfy me.

No. 3 - "Well now that is all right but a good hunter's supper would just touch the spot with me."

No. 4 - "Yes or Prairie chicken or teal duck

No. 1 - "Well a loaf of bread and milk is good enough for me."

No. 3 - "Oh! But for some worker bread and butter."

No. 2 - "Yes that would be all right with some coffee along with it all made and served by mother."

No. 4 - "Well you bet the minute I get to Honolulu or Frisco I am going to light out for a restaurant and ask them if they keep mule meat or sowbelly and if they don't I am going to stay right by them."

No. 5 - Say if you don't all shut up I get my shooting irons."

This is about the talk every night after we get to bed. We have lots of fun you bet. For my part I would like to break through one of those cellar screens and store away some of the contents of those jars over the cellar stairs.

Go up and down the quarters anytime you like during the day time you can hear what some one is going to do after pay day. All kinds of jokes are going round. Such as - we aren't going to get any money till pay day - We have not had pay day yet because they have to wait for the buglers to learn to blow Pay Day Call - We are probably going to get some money on pay day. Ask any one when pay day is coming and the answer will surely be "tomorrow." This must be so but tomorrow has been nearly two months on the road and has not got here yet.

There are quit a few from our regiment in the Brigade Hospital suffering from several diseases. Most are sent up on account of malaria or dysentery.

Co. {?} have 12 or more there and quite a few in the Regimental Hospital. There is room for about 2,000 patients at Brigade Hospital, with 15 doctors and I don't know how many nurses and stewards. There are about 500 patients there, I think. The ambulance wagon comes every day taking away severe cases from Regimental Hospital to Brigade Hospital and bringing back well ones.

Most every day Spanish soldiers (prisoners of the insurgents) break through to the American Army. They look as thought they had not been fed very well. They are kept at our guard house till further orders as to their disposal. They say Americano Mucha Grade - and think our mess is fine. They say they don't want to go back to Spain. Spain Mucha Molo (bad). One of our boys can talk Spanish and finds out mostly about the condition f the outlying country. It seems that the resources are great but everything has been neglected during the war and so the people and army are in a very bad state of affairs.

Today we had some granulated sugar mixed in with brown sugar. First I have seen since leaving *Valencia*. We had beef stake and plenty of gravy for supper last night. I think days of mule meat are over. We get fine warm biscuits three times a week. Oh! We live like lords now. And nobody has anything to say against their Uncle Samuel. I am getting so now I like tomatoes.

I am very sorry, as are all the rest of our regiment, that the regimental band could not come along with us. Every one says that there is no band here that comes up to them.

Well I don't think I will spin much more for fear you will not be able to stand it. Tell Aunt to stay for Christmas dinner for I want to find out her capacity. Wonder what capacity Father would have for Army tea? Forgot to say we get tea once a day now but it is not much like that home.

Knowing I will hear from you, but asking that Father would write as often as he can will close for this time.

From your loving Gene

American two cent stamps have run out and so you will have to pay this at your end of line. Sept. 20

September 24, 1898
Manila, Philippines

Dear Ones at Home:

No mail yet from home - it is expected about Oct. 1st. Notice is posted to effect that mail goes this morning for U.S. so I will drop a few lines as it may be sometime before another boat goes. We are all very anxious to get some kind of news from home. It has been three weeks since we got any. I generally get foreign news out of Frisco papers and local news from *Forum*. We just got news of a bad fire in Bismarck but do not know to what extent.

We got paid day before yesterday and there has been a hot time ever since. The boys are spending their money like fish buying everything and anything that takes their eye. I think I will salt some of mine away till next payday so that if we get shipped on another deal like the *Valencia* I will have some then. Drafts cannot be gotten or I would send money home. May possibly in future if I can find bill.

Yesterday the people in the cook house got into a fight (whisky) and are taking a vacation off nursing their black eyes and broken heads while three others and myself are turning out sourbelly and pancakes. This is first time in kitchen. The boys all say they get good meals and full rations.

Last evening we organized a Literary Lyceum made up of boys from the 14th Idaho and N.D. I was elected chairman protem and we had a volunteer program that was very good. I think we are going to have a good thing as it will bring the smart ones together and keep up food for thought among boys.

I have become acquainted with wealthy Spanish family and see them nearly every evening. They have a fine piano and the mistress makes good chocolate so you see I am suited. I am going to take some chocolate home when I go. It is fine.

I have been watching a Native woman for the last ten days making a fancy handkerchief. I think if Mrs. Hance could see it she would turn green. It is drawn work (think you call it) and there are pictures sowed into it. She has worked 40 days and now it most through.

Will write again hoping may get your letters before long.

Gene.

September 29, 1898
Inartel de Malatee
Manila, Philippines

Dear Father and Mother:

Just got 40 tons of mail - not I - but all of us did so you see the wheels got stopped somewhere. Got four bundles of papers: dates - *N.Y. World*- July 25–27,; *Aurgus* - July 31, Aug. 3, 5–6, 10–13, 26 and 28; *Forum* - July 25, 26, 30, Aug. 3, 6, 10–12, 25, 26; Call - Aug 3. Give my best wishes to J.J.

Letters: Father July 31 and Mother July 27 and Aug. 1 mailed Aug 2. Mother Aug 5 and 7 mailed Aug 7; J. Friedlander Aug 13 mailed Aug. 13; Mother Aug. 14 mailed Aug 14 with stamps and paper; Mother Aug 30 mailed Aug 29 with Chris Andeis letter.

Answer to Father's letter of July 31: Am sorry to again hear of your being on the sick list. I know it always makes you cross. I think Johnson did a good thing in buying the old house from Barnett. Where is the house that E.J. Moore bought? Is he intending to live in it? Give him and Mrs. Moore and the boys my best regards. You ask me about living in Honolulu. Well Honolulu is a fine place, located as it is with the far reaching Pacific to the westward and the rugged mountains at its back. The town is well kept and has many beautiful places surrounded by the tropical foliage of that latitude. However men in our regiment who enlisted from there say it is not healthy around Honolulu. The town is going to have a big boom now by parties coming from U.S. probably more than is good for it. Hasn't on an average as good business blocks as Fargo, all two stories or less and mostly of wood. Property will go up there now so that you would have to trade good for bad. I think Fargo is the best place for you except Seattle. I like Fargo and intend to make it my home.

I was down town the other day and went through the Chinese carpenter shops. They are all busy now in making boxes for the soldiers. These are of about 12" x 14" x 18" varying one way and the other. They are made of all kinds of woods such as gum wood, ebony, mahogany, teak wood, camphor wood, etc. They are dovetailed at corners and brass bound, and can be bought from 1 peso up to 20 pesos or $10. I bought one for 2 pesos or $1 and it holds everything I got and as I have always had trouble in keeping my fine pens and ink from country hayseed letter scribblers it comes in very handy. The boys seem to think what's your own is the common property of the company. They would go into my knapsack for my drill regulations and guard manual, etc.

I bought #5 sugar (granulated) at commissary for 30 cents and 1 can Eagle mild for fifteen cents, peaches for thirty cents a can, so that I can drink eight cent coffee. We get our bread from the Idahos now. They have four Dutch ovens constructed in an old unfinished fort. Their baker is a dandy and we have no kick coming on that. We trade pound for pound. When mealtime comes around I unlock my strong hold and live like a king.

I started to tell you of the Chinese workmen. I was over to a saw mill and watched them saw straight through a long log with a saw like you use on big bracket work only still larger. So far as I know this in different sizes is the only kind of a saw they have. For a plane they have a long block of wood such as an American plane with handles taken off. This they grip and plough through mahogany and ebony in some way with poor dull irons. The same would need all the strength of an American mechanic with his plane. Their chisels are short and dubby, very soft. For a mallet they use a small ax about same as your handax. They do good work though and seemingly all by guess work.

Answer to Mother's letter of July 27 No. 3: Am glad to know of you being better. I don't want you to worry anymore about me being sick for I never felt better in my life. I am getting quit a bay window on me and had to get some larger gauze shirts. You would be amazed to see the amount of American goods, the same as we get at home for sale away off here in this Spanish port where the American trade would not be patronized were it not the best. I paid twenty cents for my shirts and $1 American for a white suit of clothing to use while others are in use. Heavy office shirts are too hot so I got a couple silk shirts at fifty cents American. The felt hats are furnaces drawing all the heat and causing constant headache. I got a straw double thickness (for coolness) sombrero for twenty-five cents American. It seems strange that it is now Oct. 1 and yet I hear nothing form you to the effect that you have received any letters from me at Manila but know by way you speak you are on look out for them.

Answer to Mother's letter of Aug 5–No.5: There seems to be some more mail to come yet bringing No. 4. Am glad to know you thought of my birthday and sending 23 cents to S.S. Speaking of Mr. Coles saying that paymasters were on way and we would get pay soon - I will say if the Quartermasters and Paymasters manage things about going home we can expect it about as soon as we get pay and grub in past. Give Mr. and Mrs. Cole and Miller my best wishes. The editor of that paper which you got from Honolulu requested we give in names of all we wished to have the paper and it was sent free of charge you keep it as I have one.

Sunday Aug 7: I was on *S.S. Valencia* in Cavitte Harbor Aug. 7 and if I remember rightly wrote you a letter on that date. The day was very pleasantly spent and I hope many more may be forthcoming yet I would rather they would be at home with "Ma." You speak of rainy season making sickness, Yes it does in some cases but I haven't had a cold even and can get wet and dry out again. You speak of them harvesting wheat there, well they are harvesting peanuts here and the Manila fiber has been gathered and they are busy bailing it for shipment. The fiber is brought down the river in lighters and Chinese carry it into a large stone warehouse in which is a press run by 12 Chinese on upper floor as windless. The fiber is put in boxes or cribbing to keep it from bulging when pressure is applied, the bail is round and round and round go the poor devils till the bale is pressed enough. It is bound by long strips of rattan and carried out on shoulders of Chinese to boat. As they pass out they take a small stick painted red which they give to the tally man. This represents the number of bales per day. If they would do thins way on the bankers we would not have so many liking the climate of Mexico. You wrote you address in last letter - thought I would forget it - and liable to return home and not be able to find house.

Answer to letter from Mother Aug. 14: You write telling me that peace was declared Aug. 12 but we don't see the effects of it and I don't think we will for a good bit yet. Yet I hope I may get there soon so as to See Aunt. Give my best regards to Eunice, Abbey, Mr. and Mrs. Hansen. I have had a notion to writing to Mrs. Hiswell, but haven't got round to it. Tell her that I think of her and the "Diamonds." I am glad Aunt is keeping the rust off the coffee can till I get back. Uncle and Aunt gave me a lunch at Valley City when we went through but we had such a good time on the train that I forgot to tell you. Received stamps and paper. We can get stamps (or endorsements) by commanders.

Answer to Mother's letter of Aug. 30: You say you hope your letter will find me well. I am always well when I get letters from home and they make me feel better. The telegram from Fargo to us was read before the Battalion at retreat roll call of the day it was received. There were some loud cheers and the boys felt good. The answer - no sickness - was true to the extent that no serious cases. You speak of wishing that the U.S. only keep a coaling station here so that we can come home. I think it will be ashamed for the U.S. to give up possession to these islands after so complete a defeat as she has shown Spain. There is a great future here if the U.S. holds the Philippines with all their enormous wealth that has mostly through Spanish overbearance remained dormant or covered up. Her victories on every field of battle and also on the waters point very plainly to the fact that this is a just and righteous war and that God is on our side. I would be willing to stay my full time in a war brought on only by the neglect and ignorance of a nation who depends upon keeping things in the same old rotten rut that they are in now only by the gross ignorance of her people at large. You can see that at Santiago the people were not informed of Dewey's victory of May 1 and neither would the Officers of Manila believe of the defeat of Santiago.

Am glad to hear that the Methodists did so well in clearing themselves of debt. In reference to food will say I thing the Government has got somewhat stirred up concerning grub for we get more and better grub now and there is little kicking. You say it is lovely to have a horse and buggy. What do you mean by this? Has father purchased one? The letters from Chris Anders are interesting. I think I have said all there is to say and so will stop. Hoping the back mail and also new will reach us soon, I remain.

Lovingly, your son,
Gene

October 5, 1898
In Camp Inartel de Malates
Manila, Philippines

Dear Mother:

Your letter of Aug. 21 just received. It came in on transport ship *Scandia* and is one of the missing ones although it is not numbered. It speaks of Manila having surrendered so I suppose you knew it for some time when you wrote.

I am glad to hear that Miss Timpleton wrote to you. It shows she is a woman of her work. You speak of her being young. She is about 25 I should judge. I remember of her saying she lived in California but could not remember the address so I wrote her thanking her for the kindness shown to me while in Honolulu, and mailed it in care of Mrs. Hopper, Honolulu. I hope it reaches her. If you have her address please let me know what it is. Keep the letter with others.

The Horse and carriage mystery is cleared up in this letter by you saying that Father bought Bess.

If Fred Sawyer only know how sick I was from Frisco to Honolulu with my arm, I think she would not have expected me to write to her. As it was I did not write all I wanted to you people at home. I would like real well to be back in Fargo at the dedication of the church by Bishop Joice and also hear one Mr. Vance's grand talks again.

You speak of receiving Kodak pictures from Nellie. Did you ever send those I took?

Glad to hear of father building a house for C.B. May. He will probably get enough work now to carry him over. I would rather see him work on ship work. It is not so hard. I suppose you take your evening rides along Broadway with the rest of the stylish people. I wish I could be there to take Aunt around. Harvey says she likes riding and for that reason liked Valley City. She may stay in Fargo now. Hope she will till I get home. I am glad you have a horse for I know you will never be without one now and it will make the barn chores worth doing now. Write and tell me all about where you keep Bess, and whether or not you have the same cow. I am glad Cora is getting stone for Uncle Will and the boys. This makes me think you have never spoken of being out to Mina's grave to fix it up. I was only out there once after the stone was set. That was on my wheel and early in spring.

This makes me think of a cruel costume of the Catholic Churches here. After a person dies he is put in a vault in the cemetery and the relatives have to keep up the rent, if failing to do so the bones of that person are taken from the vault and strewn around on the ground in a "Bone yard."

At Frisco there was a lovely cemetery near our capes where they had a crematory. Their receiving vault building and chapel were simply grand. It was a good cemetery.

I have not got all of back letters yet and there are about 10 papers missing but you may have failed to send some of papers so don't look for them.

Yesterday Loyd Ryal and I were talking about going home and some very funny things were talked of. He said he could not grasp the thought of being in Fargo again. I said you bet I can and look forward to it as the supreme moment of my life when I step off the car onto the new $8,000 tile depot pavement. "Yes, says he, that pavement will be fine to see." I said don't you ever think you will see it that day. It will be literally jammed by men, women and children to greet us home. Fargo people can't be beat for receiving and they will be at their best on that day. We are all expected to get out of here by Nov. 5, so my Lieutenant told me. Let it come the sooner the better.

Now I am going to tell you something that I don't want to worry you in the least. There have three died of smallpox from our quarters (Guardel de Malatae) but as there are over 36,000 men and we have burned every bed and fumigated everything cleaned out barracks, etc. we have no fear. Doctor says I am bullet proof in that direction. The way it happened, the Spanish viciously and maligerently let the lepers and smallpox patients and all others out of the pest houses before we entered the city and they have been at large. Two have been selling pop at Malatee and have spread the disease. I don't want you to worry about this and write such dispiriting letters as you did about my arm, not that that wasn't all right for it was kind and good and motherly of you to hope for better but I don't need any sympathy or worry on your part till I get struck, then I will let you know. As I write pretty often I will keep you posted.

Gene

It would look better if you would address my letters Private instead of Mr.

October 20, 1898
Malatee, Manila
Philippine Islands

Dear Mother

376 sacks of mail from U.S. arrived and will be delivered this afternoon!!! So read the bulletin at the door of our barracks this morning and many was the anxious long after that. Well I didn't get any 376 sacks or that many letters but I did get two from you dated Sept. 2 and Sept. 9 & 19. Two from Miss Payne also clippings from her. One from Mr. Taylor. Got two bundles of papers from you. Got 6 night caps.

In your letter you speak of forming a "Red Cross Society." It is a good thing if we get what you send us. I want to thank you for the silk sleeping caps. For although I have not come in contact with any "bugs" as Mrs. Engle predicted I will always treasure it as the first present sent to me by you. I gave one to Serg't Lounden who said to than you with the best words I could use. He says he will always keep it in remembrance of the Bugs that never was. I gave another to Loyd Ryal who wanted me to kindly remember him to you. He is in a tent and says it will come handy.

In letter of Sept. 9 you tell about 1st letter from me after arriving in Philippines. I don't think it would pay me to drop a letter on the boat every day as Ed did. I wrote every time I got a chance and mailed it all at once.

I go up to see Harvey about every other day. He is as brown as a berry and healthy as a yearling calf. Give my best regards to Lyman and John. It makes me proud of Fargo to hear of the building and improvements being done there.

You go and see Mrs. Hopson and tell her that I think of her often and am so sorry to hear of her illness. I hope she will soon recover and see many a well and happy day.

You speak of writing to the "young lady who treated me so nicely in Honolulu"!! Well I am glad I struck the right girl in your sight at last. I only wish it struck her so.

Now I have gone over your letters. I want you to answer some questions. What is her address? What has become of my wheel and yours? How is my black suit getting along? I am wondering if it will grow with me.

How are the Coles getting along, also Sawyers? I have two or three unanswered letters of Blanches. Did Miss Gale McKeever come this summer? I would have renewed old acquaintances, especially with one whose picture compares with hers. Has Nig forgotten me? I haven't forgotten him. What is Wayne Eddy doing? John sings in the choir?

November 7, 1898
Figure 32: Dear Floe: This is taken in "Calle Real" or Real Avenue, near our quarters. The old cathedral in the background is St. Valentines and is our hospital and four generations old. The statue is of Queen Elizabeth and is a grand piece of work. The guard is one of the 14th Regulars. The "Muchacho" is a Philippine boy who brings me my favorite "Cacalaus" or native bananas. Of course you recognize St. E.C. Grearey Jr. Do you recognize the Spannard? John

We got our cots and mosquito netting which hang on wires over our cots. They are fine.

The mail is going now, will send a long letter to father (and any one who will want to wade through it) in a few days. I have 11 pages written now.

Write again
Give my best love to all
Gene

November 11, 1898
Cuartel de Malate
Manila, Philippines

Dear Mother:

Long have we all waited and most impatiently for the incoming of any boat which might bring mail. Every boat for the last four weeks entering the harbor or moving about in it has been called a mail boat and there has been any amount of false alarms so when the mail did come yesterday we all thought it was another false alarm.

Our company was out on outpost on an important road extending eight miles east of the city. Our men were scattered in squads along this road to keep armed parties of insurgents from passing into the American.

We have been short of men lately and especially three corporals and Sergt. Londen are in the hospital. I was placed in charge of 9 men at Block House No. 12. This is one of the many placed in the country around Manila about ½ mile apart and where every occupied by the American Army are the extreme outposts of our lines. So you see I was further out in the country (8 miles) than ever was before.

Block House No. 12 is situated in a swamp or in the midst of the hay fields. There is about a 4 mile square of open land here. The only open land near Manila. The river has been dyked up so all this land is lower than the river. Each farm is about the size of our lot and surrounded by a dike. The water may be admitted to any of these fields through a gate and thus the grass is irrigated. About eight crops a year are taken off.

But as nice as our situation was picturesquely it wasn't so nice in reality with the millions of mosquitoes and mud and water. I told you in last letter that we had been issued mosquito netting and now we never go on guard or outpost that those nettings don't go along. In fact my blanket could stay behind before I would leave this.

This is the rainy season again and the water is wet. For three days it has rained almost steady and when we got off the stone ballast roadways you bet we didn't stay on top long. The ground is sea sand and volcanic ashes making the stickiest, sloppiest, meanest mud I ever saw when it is wet. North Dakota mud can't compare with it. On the march out and back we went to our knees in mud and more a sight to see this morning. Not a dry stitch on us and mud to our very necks. I had to change everything and wash it. My body was as yellow black as though I had been dipped in a tar barrel filled with yellow ochre.

Our supper was brought out to us from quarters by an ox cart and with it came a far more important thing - mail. I forgot to eat my super and the letters and papers kept me awake all night. This was a good thing for I don't know how I would otherwise have done so. A corporal or person in charge generally has to stay on duty 24 hours instead of 2 hrs on and 6 hrs off. It rained steady all night so I was over glad to have the papers. This morning I was very sleepy but as the mail goes tomorrow I couldn't waste any time by sleeping when so many letters were to be answered.

I got two letters from you yesterday and one today. Two from Blanche and one from Isses Blanche and Mina Amerland. Besides the papers sent by you. Was sorry you didn't send papers with account of Red Cross Entertainment.

Answer to yours of Sept. 18 by kindness of Miss Frynson. You speak of my being homesick. I was while I was sick and before I received any news from you but now that I get answers to letters from here I do not feel half so long chinned. Of course we all want to get home but you know when a person is homesick he does an unnecessary amount of pining. This does no good and I have stopped it and want you too. I begin to think it would be sure death to land us in a cold country and think they ought to keep us at Frisco or Oakland till Spring.

I am beginning to think that I was weaker and thinner than I knew of for since getting well every one (even myself) thought that I weighed heavier then when I enlisted at 165, but 156 ½ so you see I have 9 lbs to put on me to get back where I was when I joined. I never want to be vaccinated again. The other day the doctor vaccinated every one over again. I told my 1st Sergt I didn't want to be stuck again but he said I had to fall in with the rest. The Doc put me in a easy state of mind when I went to strip off by saying - "Hell!, I never want to look at your arm again, I saw it enough on the *SS Valencia*" and so you see while the others have sore arms I can boast f as healthy a system as any soldier in the army. But my left arm is a bad looking sight. For about 8" along the upper arm the muscle is slurfed away natural result the left arm is still weak.

The pajama suits which you speak of making come in very handy as the less clothing a person wears the better off he is. Every one in the Hospitals should have one, instead of night gowns.

How was each face shown in Shelock Lodge Picture? In what pictures were mine shown? Harvey told me quite awhile ago that Bertha expected to get married and about their new house. I read all his letters and he reads mine this making news go farther.

Answer to Estra letter enclosing the one intended to be sent by the Red Cross nurse. About the amount of sickness here will say that the statement sent from here are false and I will wager that the percentage of sickness in the N.D. troops is 35% at present. I don't want to scare you but when I get home I want facts to look at in my own letters. The smallpox is almost subsided two of the boys from our company are acting as nurses there. There is a hospital for 1,000 men here and they have to place some in tents and in another building. That is only our own Brigade. There are others as warm as us.

We got paid last Tuesday and voted the same day for state ticket. Republican in our company.

I notice you always expect letters from me and when you get them your letters are of a more cheerful cast. Of course this is natural but you must remember connections are very poor between here and the U.S. so no regular mail goes.

I am glad to hear father has so much work on hand. "All things come to those who wait" and I suppose he will have more than he wants from now on.

You want to know about cooking and washing. Well we are talking about hiring a Chinese cook as our present one is not entirely satisfactory. Our grub is good and plentiful but is not served up in just as clean a manner as one would like. We have tomatoes, rice, prunes, real potatoes, fresh meat, smoked ham, home made bread (made by baker in H) once in awhile cake and gravy, beef soap, oatmeal, raised biscuit, Boston Baked beans, canned beef and tongue, eggs (in place of meat) tea, coffee, etc. etc. Of course we do not have all at once but enough change to keep our appetites up and keep us healthy.

My washing is done by a Native woman. She is excessively neat and does each piece for 2 ½ cents Americano. This is cheaper and cleaner and more healthy for my knapsack as I keep everything clean. Then whenever I go on guard I generally get "orderly" on account of my cleanliness. So you see I do keep clean and respectable without your digging into my ears.

Answer to Sept. 25: It seems queer to have you talking about cold weather and Xmas. That free present ship to us boy us is a good joke. I hope it is a practical one.

I am glad you sent towel and netting although netting won't come into use unless I loose my already neatly made net which hangs over me at night.

Answer to Sept. 27: Stating that you had just received two letters from me. The stamps come in handy. I subscribed for *Chronicle* for 3 months so suppose you don't get it anymore. I don't drink ½ pint of water a day so don't worry on that point. Sometimes paper is scarce so I always save all I get hold of and try to write to you on small size as it will all be the same in a file. I use any size to others. Stamps are scarce sometimes and then I have to send letters without them. Will settle bills when I get home. I have not finished yet as I don't want to go by guess work.

I often wonder who runs the washing machine and lawn mower, who slams the door, who throws their cap around, who covers up the flower pie plant, who pokes Nig in the ribs, who eats up the sugar, who washes the windows, and puts them on, and who breaks them. Who takes down carpets, who leaves the doors unlocked at night, who makes the ice-cream and who eats it, who stores the vegetables away, who goes up and down stair six steps at a time, who eats the currents and raspberries, who keeps the ditches free from weeds, who chitters up the shop, who stinks up his clothes for two months after fixing celery, who keeps the gasoline stove going, who keeps his room and all the other rooms in the house full of his cobwabbled up jim cranks, - well do you blame a fellow if he wants to get back up to his neck in the jamjar, sugardrawer, raisin box, cracker bag, steal the cakes, hook the cookies, munch apples, carrots, turnips, !!! Hiptet-Hi-Yi Ten Quart Kittleson Ole Overhalson Hoopalah! Well we are coming home some day and then you won't know Fargo. Oh say! Do you smell onions? Well excuse me, but I am eating young ones and if you don't like it just hold the letters a little further away. But fever and onions won't go in same letter so the fever won't for the onions have got it. See.

Speaking about Alcess discharging 12 gts will say I always thought I had about 10 qt capacity but didn't think it had reached that prodigious capacity.

Well mail goes in morning and I must close now-taps. Excuse my writing as I have pushed per all day.

Gene

November 24, 1898
Manila, Philippines

Dear Mother:

Boat does not leave till tomorrow so will add a few lines more.

The largest mail that has ever been on the Pacific Ocean leaves here today or tomorrow. There is so much that only the registered mail is put in regular U.S. mail sack. The other is put in gunny sacks and half of it will not get to its destination.

For this reason I registered all your mail that has presents in it.

I sent a bamboo case with a spoon, flag, and powder in it. The bamboo case I cut in the woods, so it is green and strong. The spoon is one made by a Native here and will be a curiosity to you undoubtedly. The powder is for father. He can carry this instead of tobacco in his pocket. It is perfectly safe. I have burned lots of it and it burns about like a match when first lighted. It is the best kind of powder for safeness there is and is far superior to the used in the U.S.N. I got it from the magazine of one of the large Krupp Guns 10" at the Lunatas, the might. I was corporal of the guard at that place. The flag is a Spanish Coat of Arms and father may use it for his Sunday handkerchief. I am trying to get a Filipino flag.

The handkerchief I sent you in the registered letter is one I ordered from a Native woman to make for you and the cloth is handmade of a peculiar goat's hair. She made it all. This piece of work is worth a small fortune in America and I don't think there are many better. The word mother I had to mark for her as that was "Americano" all the rest is her own design. I sent the Eddy girls some shawls that were pretty but cheap.

I am looking for something for Miss Payne that can be sent in a letter and may not get it off on this boat so tell her not to worry. This is Thanksgiving day and we do not have to drill. Will close now with a Merry Xmas.

Gene

December 1, 1898
Manila, Philippines

Dear Mother:

This is the first day of the last month in '98, yet how unlike December it seems here; warm as I ever saw it in the States-rain every day-summer attire worn-grass the greenest, trees the leafiest, and all nature at its best. The seasons here are a puzzle to me. There is little or no change in temperature, rain everyday, hot sun also. The wind comes from the northeast now where it once came from the southwest when we first came. I did not receive any mail from you on this last boat, but as the *Indiana* is expected in any time, I hope to get news from you before this mail closes. The *Indiana* is five days over due now.

I do not know what to write. There is nothing of importance going on. The Thanksgiving passed off very quietly. Orders were issued allowing soldiers a holiday from the drill. In our company we did not have anything extra for dinner, as there has been some trouble about the Company fund. Every other company in the regiment and in Manila had something extra for dinner. I was invited by Floyd Ryal over to Co. D for dinner. It was very fine, and by far the best I have had here. There was chicken and gravy with dumplings (your style) mashed potatoes and radishes. Pie (apple) and pears. I don't think you could beat that unless you had one of Mrs. Farrell's "turkeys." My correspondence is steadily increasing.

This just suits me. It takes up my spare moments in reading the letters and papers sent and answering back.

I received a very interesting letter from Frank Knerr which told of the S.S. Brass and Y.M.C.A. in a very interesting manner. In it were some excellent "Kodak" views of the new depot-Electric Light works-3 new stores on Broadway. In one could be seen the unfinished hotel on the Sherman corner.

I got a letter from Mrs. Matson, my traveling companion from Seattle to Valley City. Excuse me for writing here [across the top margins of letter] but taps will blow in a second and I must close.

Gene

December 2, 1898
Manila, Philippines

Dear Ones at Home:

This is a continuation of last nights letter. The Indiana got in last night and I got two letters from Mother of Oct. 17 and 19. Also large bundle of papers. Got letter from Mrs. Latimer also a paper from her and a letter from Archie Cone.

I will take up your letters first. Oct. 17: You say you received only a few letters from me. I know I am irregular, but will try to be more regular in the future. I will commence and number all mine, you do same. Then we will know whether we skip any. I am recording on envelopes of all letters received the date they come. I love to have the rest of the people write to me and hope you will not think I am neglecting you. If Mrs. Laizure had been here when I received her letter I am afraid I would have made Mr. Laizure jealous.

Frank Andrs was in the Division hospital with diareah but is on duty now after quire an illness.

Harry Berry received quite a few letters from the Stilwells. He calls them father and Mother and seem very much attached to them. By the way he has worked things so we have a very good band now. But none I have seen or heard comes up to the Band. However they have push.

I have written letter to John but I have never received reply. Will try it again with his address you sent.

We are all looking for those Xmas boxes, though it is early yet.

You must not think I forget Aunt just because I do not write to her. She is included in "Dear Ones at Home.

I have to chop off now to get to bed. Will finish tomorrow.

Gene

December 2, 1898
Manila, Philippines

Dear Ones at Home:

You only have to come for hot weather and you can have all you want. Yes he is the same old Archie. His letter to me is a good one but you would never dream that he had any folks. Never says anything except that Bob went west.

Answer to Oct. 19: Never mind sending socks, etc. - can buy anything. I commenced shaving so don't let this trouble you. I am gathering a few "curios" to take home as you suggest.

You speak of tying "comforter" with Aunt. It if were here you would want to tie it with ventilating holes.

You ask how hot it is here. I don't know but do know that persons in the hospital often have a temperature of 107° without being considered dangerous. This, I suppose, is due to the hot climate.

Requisitions for clothing gets the articles very quickly now. So we have all the clothes we want.

Oct. 22 same letter: Do send pictures of yourself and Aunt and be sure to keep her on ice till we return. Harvey wishes to see her very much. Hi is in command of "G" now. I read all his letters and he reads yours.

We had dress parade yesterday and looked very fine. We should have two a week but the rain has interfered for three weeks.

It is 8:30 and I will close hoping you are all well and contented.

Give my best regards to all, especially to Dallas, Herb, Jerome, Bennie, Harold, Paul Halley, Lilian, and the rest of the kids that used to play in my yard.

Gene

December 6, 1898
Manila, Philippines

Dear Mother:

Yesterday we were out on outpost so I could not write any. I have got a very lame ankle caused by stepping on a round stone. I am packing in lineament and the pain is going away.

Tomorrow I am on guard and may not get time to write any. However, it is 4 hours off, 2 one and if I can get away from the guard house will write you something.

Things are getting into better shape now. We are beginning to reap the benefits of the kicks made in the U.S. concerning the care of soldiers. Cargoes now arriving have a better class of gods in them. Many things are issued which were left out before-such as syrup, canned "Boston Baked Beans", corn beef, fresh onions, radishes, and potatoes, etc., etc. The clothing issue is fully up to Government too now. Blue blouses are of good material and make up. I received my first pair of real government shoes just the other day and they are fine. Not a tack or nail to bother the feet, and not made on Spanish style to press the toes and blister the heel. I have always gone without a double change on account of shabbiness of goods, but now have put in an order for quite an amount of extra clothing.

The Colonel says that we will all be allowed to take boxes home with us so we can store extra clothing.

There is a great deal of talk going on among the boys about going down south to another island. However as only regiment is to go and as ever regiment in Manila is sure that they are going, I don't think we will go.

Good by for tonight,
Gene

December 7, 1898
Manila, Philippines

Dear Mother:

Today I am on guard and have post No. 3. This is at the back of the Guard House and is a good place to see the shipping. I was on guard from 12:00 to 2:00 and saw the *Puebla* as she came in. We expect she has quite a bit of mail on board for us. I knew her as soon as she turned broadsides at the mouth of the harbor 27 miles away. Just think of watching a boat coming from Wheatland to Fargo at 2:00 p.m. and you got the exact position and time but not the grand waste of rolling illons between.

You should see the crowds on the beach every time a boat comes in. It means mail and as there are about 28,000 mail hungry soldiers in Malate Barracks you will see just about that number on the beach.

No more news just now so will quit for a time.

Dec. 8, 1898: Mail got in last night at 6:00 p.m. One letter from you of Oct. 28 also bundle of papers, letter from Mrs. Latimer of Nov. 5 saying she had sent me a Christmas box and a book from Miss Minnie A. Gibbons entitled "The Prince of the House of David" by Rev. J.H. Ingraham. It is about the same kind as "The Tale of the Christ" and "The Restler of Phillip." These are good-cheap books and I wish more could be distributed among the boys.

I saw two more boats come in this morning at 2:00 a.m. but a fog has come down and we don't know what they are. I think one is the *Newport*. I am going to sleep now.

Gene

December 9, 1898
Manila, Philippines

Dear Mother:

Mail goes to Hong Kong at 10:00 a.m. this morning so will drop a few lines to be sure you get one and Mrs. Geary don't get ahead of you. I suppose I could write a letter everyday and drop it in the box but somehow I don't think it would be so interesting. However I don't like to read of you not getting letters.

I was up to see Lt. Geary about transferring from Co. A to Co. B. He spoke to me quite awhile ago about it and has been waiting till John McCannel got his discharge. Yesterday Taylor Gruin's son was up and wanted to be enlisted into Co. B but Lt. Geary said he would rather have me and anyway I came in first. Young Erinn bunked his way on a sailing vessel here to join the army.

Last night I put in an application for a transfer and Lt. Newcomber signed it. All that is needed now is for the Cols. Signature. Lt. Geary said he would tickle the Col. Up to sign it this morning. So soon I expect to tell you to address my letters to "B" instead of "A".

Your pictures were all right for samples hope you will send on the good ones someday. At least as good as the "Kodak" view.

The funny cracks you send livened the boys up quite a bit. Send some more.

I don't know what more to write. Lt. Newcomber is talking to me now and says he came near not signing my release from this company as he is so short of men.

John McKinnel of "B" and Edward Fay, Jr., of "A" have their discharges and leave for Fargo soon.

I will give them letters of introduction to you and hope they will see you. Use them well for me. Mail is closing.

Gene

December 10, 1898
Manila, Philippines

Dear Mother:

I will write a few more times to you so that you will be sure and have one next time the mail arrives.

We are all waiting for news from Congress now that it is met. We hope that they will see fit to send us home as soon as possible. That would mean that we would be on the road home about the 1st of April so that we could land in Fargo sometime in May. This would satisfy us quite well. One can't go anywhere in Manila but he hears soldiers talking of the time when they are going home. There are as many different opinions and rumors as there are men.

I have not got any news concerning my transfer from "A" to "B" as yet, but hope to have before I close up this letter. I will be very glad to be up with the town boys. As it is now, to see them or Harvey I have to go about ½ mile and it is rather unhandy. I will only be a block from Harvey then.

The "Blue Book" of the U.S. Army says a soldier may be transferred from one company to another in the same regiment for coject reason only.

A written application most be signed by the company commanders and the colonel. As a coject reason I said that Co. B was my home town Company and that I thought that I could serve the U.S. in a better capacity in that Company. However, I had more reasons that this for transferring. Co. "B" is the best Company so every one says and Lt. Geary is a good Officer.

I will stop for awhile and finish later.

4:00 p.m., Dec. 10: Well here I am in Co. "B" not quite settled yet but hope to be before long. I had to leave gun, belt, bayonet, knapsack, haversack, canteen, shelter tent, meat pan and cup in Co. "A" and have not drawn any in Co. "B" yet. I am quartered in a fine room just across the hall from Tad Foster and Dan Lewis. My roommates are-Frank Anders, Frank Newman (who used to go to the N.D.A.L.), Louis Anderson (worked in N.P. Shop) and Jim Magugen (N.D.A.C. boy). They are all nice boys and we have a great time together.

The "chuck" up here is not quite as good as in Co. "A" but I didn't come for that.

All the boys shook my hand and say they are glad to see me where I belong.

There is a fine shower bath with a marble tub and a fine patent (pressure) water closet. As fine as in any place in Fargo. My room is on second floor facing South and East. Just below us there is a fine flower garden with all kinds of tropical growth.

I will close for tonight. May add more in the morning. Tomorrow is Sunday. From

Private E.H. Sacket
Co. B, 1st N.D. Vol.
Manila, Philippines

December 11, 1898
Manila, Philippines

Dear Mother:

Well I have passed my first night as a Company "B" boy and for some reason or other I slept very well. Every bit of noise ceased at tops and it did not take me long to get to sleep. Down in the other quarters noise kept up all night. Everything is done in military manner here. The officers have a snap and go to them.

Just after breakfast I received my guns and other acotraments and I have been busy most of the morning in getting things into shape.

3:30: Well I had a good dinner and a short nap. Then I went and had a fine bath, the text since being on the islands, so you may feel rejoiced that this afternoon you won't have to dig out my ears.

Tuesday Dec. 13: Yesterday I was on outpost or guard-as we call it-so did not write any. There are 9 guards out of the company each morning. We and "G" mounting guard together. "G" furnishes 5 men. I think this guard is better than at the other place as all we have to have clean is our gun. Down there we had to have our shoes polished, leggins brushed, wear white pants, blue coat, and wear it all day in the heat. Yesterday I was out with an old pair of brown pants and a gauze shirt. I will close now and drop this in the mail box.

Gene

December 15, 1898
Manila, Philippines

Dear Mother:

We are having delightful weather just now. It has not rained for about a week and the sun is not so very hot.

Yesterday we drilled on extended order, or skirmish drill, out through the entrenchments and it was rough and ready work indeed. Lt. Geary knows his business and it is a pleasure to work under him. Co. B goes through movements that officers of other companies know little or nothing about. Yesterday the mail came in but I did not get any letters from Fargo-only one-from W.H. Day of Tacoma. He writes a good letter. I have a bundle of Manila papers already to send home to Father. These I wish him to keep till I get home and I will have something valuable.

I am on guard tomorrow so can not write much just now.

Let. Newcomber of Co. A just was here and left me a Xmas package. It was made of tin and was 7 ½" x 9 ½" x 5 ½". Articles contained: Face Towel large, Dish Towel large, 24 Envelopes, 2 fine Keystone Tablets (worth more than all the rest), 1 comb-this is my 5th, and last but not least, One large piece of fruitcake which all the boys said was very fine. It was just as fresh as the day it was baked.

Evidently the officers think that the natives are going to attack us. We are doubled up on post every night and there are two extra post away out from the fort. As it was there were only about 9 men now there are about 28 or 30 on guard often.

I think however we will soon settle the Filipinos and then duty will be easier.

Dec. 16: Tomorrow I am on guard again. There seems to be no trouble but yet we are prepared for anything that comes.

I am getting more to do in this Co. and like it better. "The Devil finds work for idle hands."

We have a 6 foot table in our room so I have a nice place to draft.

Dec. 17: Did not get on guard today. Just got two boxes from Mrs. Latimer weighing 40 lbs. In one was a year's of *Colliers Weeklys*. They were fine-showing pictures of the war. These are the first of illustrated weeklies we have seen here and were very interesting. Besides these were 6 large bottles of "Sosaparill and Iron" which all declared excellent. In other box was a large fruitcake, checker board (just the ticket) about 2 lbs candy and 2 lbs nuts, package of rolled oats, writing tablets-handkerchiefs, envelopes, pens, pencils, etc.-all to be divided between Bert Grafton and myself.

I must close now will drop you another soon.

Gene
Co. B

FIGURE 33: Envelop by Eugene Sackett.

December 19, 1898
Manila, Philippines

Dear Mother:

Was on guard yesterday so could not write you. Am now using the first sheet of paper went me by Mrs. Lattimer.

No mail has come in yet but the *S.S. St. Paul* is expected daily. I got a letter on the last mail from Mr. Day and Miss Gibbons of Tacoma. None from you.

There is nothing to tell you about this place. The Filipinos watch us and we them just like two little boys.

Frank Anders and I are up to our old tricks of studying like at home. I have sent to Frank Kneir for my geometry so that I may pick up and also give Frank a brushing. I keep drawing most of my spare time and Maj. White has me at work now on a large map of the trenches so that he will know where he is at. It is simply an accommodation.

Dec. 20: This is a fine day and there are a lot of visitors out to the fort looking for mouzer bullets (that are not there).

Harvey was over this morning to see my Xmas box. I guess he wanted some of the bottles but I didn't think they were good for him and so didn't offer to divide. He is good and homesick and would walk home if he had a chance.

Dec. 21: I was down to the Luneta last night and listened to a concert given by the Colorado Regimental Band. There were 56 pieces and the music was very fine. Both comical and patriotic.

Gen Aguissaldo sent a note to Gen. Otis that he ('ag') could not restrain his men longer from entering Manila. Otis sent word back "Gen Aguissaldo dear Sir: Let them come. I need some street cleaners. Gen. Otis." So you see I have no chance to show my bravery or lack of same. I am n guard again tomorrow.

Dec. 22: Mail arrived. Got letters from you dated No. 5-10-14, from Emma MacLein, Mrs. Lattinice, Rev. Vance, bundle of town papers and Scientific Americans from you. Am on guard and can't say much.

Dec. 23: Just got off guard and am very sleepy so will sleep till noon and then write a little. 2 p.m.: Answer to yours of Nov. 6: You remember what you told me concerning Eddy's getting 6 letters all in one day. Well I have been Tad's room and joshed him pretty hard about it, but of course he pleaded not guilty.

Am glad that you are making a mattress for me as this is the first of those much needed articles which you have made for me.

There is no use in Edward's writing as he does for by the time his letters are in the *Forum* the matter is long over here and causes you undue worry when there is no need of it.

You could not have suited me better in sending the Building Supplement of the *Scientific American* as I long for these things but never mind sending any more of the other as they are expensive and the subjects treated are not in my line.

The town papers, as you say, are not good for much about Election time.

Yes, I got drawing of Nig's foot and acknowledged the same some time ago. I think also knight caps-netting, towel, etc.

Now you speak of money question again, as you have every letter yet. I am getting tiered of it as there is not enough money in this business to worry about. You say-save your money till you get home so you can have a good time. Well now that way I look at it, as do any of us, that to get in the U.S. again will be good time enough for us. What little money we have to spend here makes things a little better for us.

Now about that Spanish Family, don't worry as they say they never had such good times as now.

When Harvey says I am homesick I would like to ask what do you call it with him. I am fat, healthy and good natured. Harvey is poor and goes around whining about home all the time.

No more letters without stamps can be sent so stamps come in handy.

Now, tomorrow is inspection so I must close and shine up.

Day after tomorrow is Christmas day coming on Sunday. Every one says I am lucky in the X Box affairs.

As a suggestion I wish you would keep a note book of those who speak of me and letters received and sent. Again I say please write plainer!!! I had an awful time in making out your pencil letter.

Gene
Co. A

December 23, 1898
Manila, Philippines

Dear Mother:

Here is a hand made handkerchief that I saw made by a Filipino woman.

Just got two letters and bundle of papers from you.

Mail to U.S. goes 10 a.m. now goes and have to go to town and get this registered.

May not get it on this boat.

Gene
Merry Xmas.

December 23, 1898
No. 14, Co. B, 1st N.D. Vol.
Manila, Philippines

Dear Father:

Your welcome letter of Nov. 8 received. I always look for letters from you every mail but they seldom come. Fool trash is all right just send some more. I see that you still stick to that pessimistic idea of working on holidays and election day. If all such men as you stay away from the poles as you do things will soon go to the devil.

Your horse and cow talk was all right and interesting. If you could be induced to come over there I would gladly speak of money a good many times. You ask if there is no better place than Fargo. I think you would be foolish to move away from there now. However, if you could only see what we have seen it would be very nice. This is no place for a working man or one without money unless he is a Chinese. A carpenter would have to learn his trade all over again, few buildings will ever do me any good in Architectural work when I get back. All the lumber is delivered in large timbers at the new building and is whip sawed by Chinese into the kind of boards wanted. You will see at once that is a slow and tedious way taking us back to the day when there was no dimension lumber. Every piece that is wanted for finishing work must be smoothed up with an old plan which can't hold a candle to oldest "jack" plane of yours.

The house we are quartered in is very nice and large and took fifteen year to build. It cost 50,000 pasos ($25,000).

Dec. 25: Well Christmas has almost gone and as I am watching the red sun disappear in all its glory behind Corrigedore Island I will tell you how I fared. I think I got more than if I had been at home, but neverless I would rather be there.

Mrs. Latimer sent me two boxes - one with 6 bottles of Cider and Ginger ale and almost 6 months of *Collier's Weeklys*. There were fine and we all enjoyed them. The other box had candy, nuts, books, cakes, checker board, writing tablet, pencils, envelopes. The cakes kept fine especially the fruitcake. I got a box from Bismark made of tin. In it were pencils, letter paper, envelopes, fruitcake, two towels, and nuts.

Best of all I got a large box from home with so many good things in it - not trashy things but common sense ones. The bandages were made very nice and will be worn. The shoe laces are great deal better than those the Gov. furnishes and in this damp climate the best are needed. The safety pins and needles and thread will come in very handy. I think when I look at the nuts that the box of candy must have come from you. It was fine.

The Spanish are no people for such nice things. The pictures of Mrs. Pearson and Jerome are very good. The tablet is the size I like and is of good paper. I have about 12 towels, now, and in this warm climate where nightly baths are taken a goodly number are needed.

The camphor will keep my knapsack in fine condition. The chewing gum is doing a glorious work for the country. The handkerchiefs I use for my neck to keep away sorethroat. I have never had a sorethroat since being on the island. We have lamps so the candles will be kept for future use.

The lead pencil and especially the rubber bands are all right. They will help to hold my letters. Tell Aunt that I have looked all over Manila for an indelible pencils so that she struck the right spot in sending me one. The soap will be used in time (however, I have 6 bars of Ivory now-and you know that is good enough for me). Thank Mrs. Luizure for that cake of Sour Milk compliction sweetener and tell her that I hope to return as white as a lily (nit-you ought to see me).

The handkerchiefs that Blance sent me will only be displayed on grand state occasions. They are very nice but Mucha Blanka (too white). Miss Payn's present was very nice but the ribbons look too nice to untie so I will leave them folded.

That picture of Jerome was a cracker jack and I have it pasted on my had along with the rest of my family group so that I have my friends out on guard with me. I suppose before this Old Mrs. Pearson has had her windows snugly fitted so that I may not bother about that. Her picture was fine.

The picture of Payn's house was good and made me think how much nicer the northern foliage is then this tropical brush.

Last night I went in swimming and took a shower bath afterwards. The sea is very salty in tropical countries and keeps a person up. It is warm and nice. After being in the water a while we got up in the soft sand of the sea beach and played tag, leap-frog, ran races, and rolled in the sand, you bet we were dirty when we got through.

You will think this is a funny thing for me to go swimming on Christmas Eve. Well yes it is the first and probably the last time I will ever do such a thing on Christmas Eve.

Night before last I was on guard and it was very, very cold. I had on undershirt and drawers, blue shirt, brown suit, and overall a rain coat and poncho. I look at the thermometer to see if the Bay would be frozen over for Xmas day and it was 76° above. I suppose if you could have a day once in a while as warm as that you would be satisfied.

For dinner to day, we had chicken with dressing, mashed potatoes, good brown gravy, radishes, tea, coffee, peach pie. 10 pounds candy from Erhman, 2 boxes of cigars from Bowers. For supper O.Y.S.T.E.R.S. gotten out of Manila Bay. Now did you beat that.

I must close now as Uncle Sam will get poor if he has to carry much more of my trash.

Hoping to hear from you soon, I remain
Lovingly
"Skunewagg"
Co. B

December 28, 1989
Manila, Philippines

Dear Mother:

I haven't much to write but will send you a word or two. Christmas is over and we are all feeling good. We had to go on "Dress Parade" today but it was call on the sight of the parade of the 14th Regulars was well worth our going down there.

"Guard Duty" is heavy now. I just came off this morning. However I would rather by a long shot be here then down with "A".

The rain is coming again and the nights are cold. Mail is expected daily but I guess that it will be about 2 weeks before we get any. If it did not cost so much I would send it by Hong Kong and Van Gonver and ask you to do the same then we could each get a letter once a week. As it is Uncle Sam's service is bum.

Yesterday I saw a Thomas Lawn Mower and last night I dreamed that I was just knocking the high places off the lawn at home. Taps are blowing so I will "quite."

[letter ends with a drawing of him in bed and mowing the lawn]

January 1, 1899
Manila, Philippines

To All at Home:

Well here we are on this beautiful Sunday morning, ushered into the glories of the last year of the 19th Century, amid flowers and ferns-palms and tropical growth of every description. It is winter now-the thermometer going as low as 65° at night and I can tell you as we stand guard we need all the clothes that Uncle Sam gives us.

I was on guard last night from 11 p.m. 1898 to 1 a.m. 1899 and so guarded two whole years in the same night. Every boat in the harbor blew its whistle, every church in the city rang its bell ad canons were fired.

Now I will answer some of your letters. Three from you were received Dec. 30 also bundle of papers. Today Red Cross nurse sent me another letter with clothes and money in it. Answer to yours of Dec. 16: Don't every think I am homesick for I am not. Give best regards to Mrs. Wiswell and tell her I love her as I did long-long ago.

I write to so many that time is well taken up but will try to get one to her some of these days also to Mr. Cole.

I wish you would not write so about Uncle Russel's folks and Aunt for Harvey and I exchange letters and it is not the most pleasant to either of us.

You tell father the skating out here is good as h----. Concerning washing I do all my own except the white suits.

Answer to yours of Nov. 18: Condensed milk don't cut much figure here as I like my coffee as well clear. Yes, between the lying papers and the lying 13th Min. you people are led to believe all kinds of things. There isn't a man in Manila that has any use for the 13th outside of themselves. To hear them talk you would think they did it all-when in fact they run away and left the Astor Battery to their fate in the battle. The Astors left (not long ago) for N.Y. and to give people here a true opinion of the 13th stacked out in the road in front of their guarters 27 guns that they had picked up and which the 13th had thrown away in their flight in battle. On the stack was pined: "27 rifles thrown away by the Glorious 13th Min. on the day of the battle." It made the 13th pretty mad. The Astors say had it not been for the "N.D." they would not have been able to recapture their small cannon.

My work with pen only lasted a few days and did not excuse me from duty. In this country I don't care for that kind of work as there is no exercise. Letter writing is enough.

Give my best to R.N. Johnson and tell him I hope he will be on his feet before this reaches home. You bet. You say the schools have been closed on account of sickness-well we are better off here-I guess.

Grandma Roffins and also Mr. Roffins have my best regards. I'll never forget how she would examine my face and then say "Why! Is this you, Gene". Concerning the printing of letters. To see so many misstated letters about matters here, printed in the papers, makes one have that tired feeling. Sometimes I have written letters home that tell of something I have seen. I have seen such war ships. Such letters I am willing to let you do as you please but most of them I write to you and not for everyone.

You speak of telephone for Vance-wish you had one for I think I could understand you better than I can be letter. You would put in periods better.

Answer to yours of Nov. 22: Yes Wort Wilson had a pull and went home when sick boys who were trying for a discharge in his own company had to stay.

It is not to be wondered amongst so many soldiers 20,000 that one dies a week. Would like to have you point out any place in the world where death rate is less. Insurance companies would have a snap here.

By the way you never speak of any insurance-how it come out?

Kodak films are not good here and I think Tad will have to hustle if he gets good pictures. I have no interest in Camera on account of what you said to me that pictures would be a poor investment.

Answer to letter sent by nurse who arrived on boat of Dec. 29 but whose trunk was left on boat till Jan. 1 so that just got letter. Thanks for rags, money, $4.00 arrived safe and will get something. I have never seen the nurse and so can not say that I liked her. She brought a telegraphic code to Co. B plus $25 for messages. We sent one this morning. You tell May that letter to Emma was a Corporation affair and that I did not dare venture a letter to her. I will in near future.

You are foolish again to think Harvey would try to take Co. clerk away from me. It was my own doings any way he and I are the best of friends. I don't see how Mrs. Carpenter remembers me as I never spoke to her in my life that I know of. You speak of Lyman at Hong Kong - wish I could go that way back for they say it is beautiful.

You speak of the nurse having a hard time here. Well may be they do but we never see it. Any time you like you can see them out riding with some officer on the Luneta. I think I spoke of mosquito netting - towel-caps, etc. as soon as received. Never try to send jelly for I fear it would break, but next Xmas please send large enough fruitcake to make up for one you did not this year. The handkerchief you got for Xmas was the one spoke of the woman working 40 days at. Never mind what it cost. You needn't sell if for less than $20.00. I will send some cheap things some day.

Now about the *Harpers Weekly* letter. I exercise a great deal every morning and evening, and take a nap every day.

You must know that Dan Davis of Coperstown is a nurse in Hospital and I have never seen him since we were on the boat.

Every letter that you write gets harder to make out and read than the one before it. In last letter, for instance you write like this "there is to be a (can't make out word!) at D-Linderise Hall given by High School girls Clyde got an invitation and Carie Eddy names heads the list Mrs. Luizure says the expense is borne by the young ladies that will suit Clyde Mrs. Geary and two younger children is at Casseltore visiting her mother the address is Miss Lena Templeton Pasadena C." Now this is very good news but too long a sentence. I want to save your letters so I will have them in after years so Please Write Plain. Don't get offended at me, but buy a note book and do as I do. Set down the things you want to speak of and settle them all up before you go on to the next. I have an outline of nearly every letter I have written so that I know what I wrote last.

I got letters from Ellis Fisher, Frances Fritchie, 2 from Blanche. All ere good especially Frances as she gave me all the University news.

I will close now as I have filled too many pages already and have no more to tell.

Gene

Letters From Manila— Inland Campaign
January 13, 1899 to June 2, 1899

January 13, 1899
Manila, Philippines

Dear Father:

I have not written since the 1st and good reasons-no time. The Filipinos are getting a little to fresh again and as a result we have to scratch gravel. There is not much use in telling about it as the papers before this (at home) are full of it. These people are not to be trusted an inch. A short time ago old Aqinauldo agreed to lay down his arms if the U.S. held the islands. About a week ago he issued a proclamation to the people stating that the U.S. is not doing by them what it ought and advised them to accept their protection here only for the present. The old fool was feeling the U.S. for some money. Two days he was so bold as to post up notices in Manila asking all Filipinos and "respectable" consuls to recognize and help the revolutionary government and signed his name as president. Now he declares that the only way the U.S. can take possession of these islands is to make him the Gov. Gen.

Now we would not care if we could only sleep at night and not be called out more than twice a day, but in the contrary we are forced to sleep in our clothes not even removing our leggins. It has been 110 hrs now since I have had my shoes off and my feet are in a bad shape.

We have been called into the trenches time and time again only to find that it is only a scare. Day before last about 1:30 a.m. a drunken bugler got hold of a bugle on the Escolta and blew "to arms" (the call used in case of a sudden attack). Well inside of ten minutes every man all over Manila a distance of ten miles, was in the trenches.

About 8 p.m. a badly scared sentinel at the fort came and reported that three were all of 25 Filipinos advancing on his post. Co. B was in the trenches in no time and the *Monaduc* came over from Cavite and made thing lighter than day by her search lights. She has been stationed here and is only 1000 yards from our quarters. We have a great time hearing the [?] and bells on board.

Last night an attack was expected and we were all on the alert. Nothing has happened and we are allowed to breath the warm air of another day in the tropics.

We do sentinel duty now with loaded rifles and allow no one to pass the lines at night. Last Sunday we (B & G) worked hard all day to repair up the walls and put up entrenchments on top. It was hard work carrying the heavy stones. Monday the rest of the 1st battalion threw up a new line of trenches near the fort.

FIGURE 34: Nebraska Out-post attached by Filipinos.

FIGURE 35: Montana Boys on Out-post duty, P.I.

Pay day has come and gone and same with most of the money. It is strange how some people can think that we can save money (15.60 per month pay) to have a good time on when we get home. We have little enough to spend on an occasional dinner or trip of sight-seeing. It is a fact that for want of money the boys can see the great battle ships under their very nose, when if they had been home and those same ships had been 20 miles away they would have broken their necks to get to see them. I keep $10 ahead for return trip expenses or for case I would be taken sick. Last Friday I went and got some drawing paper. Hunted all over Manila for a print shop where they kept good goods. At last found one about 7 miles from quarters that was a buster. The building covered as much room as both buildings of the N.P. machine shops. Everything in the way of printing or book binding could be done. There were about 30 Lithographing presses and 75 printing presses. Everything crowded. Got some good paper and will send some sketches home soon.

Frank Anders is taking drawing lessons from me, and we have plenty to do in quiet spells. Have not done anything in quiet spells, however, for the last few days but sleep. I am going to roll in now for a nap.

Good By,
Will Write Again
Gene

January 23, 1899
Manila, Philippines

Dear Mother:

Just heard that mail for U.S. closes today and I will write a few lines hoping to get them in. Received your letter of Nov. 25 on Jan 19, also papers.

Sorry but not surprised that Mrs. Payne is dead. She was well along in years.

You speak of not receiving mail when other do. That is because a ship generally sails for the U.S. so soon after the posting of the bulletin regarding her departure that we do not get time to write.

Mail has been coming in about once a week and I haven't got but one letter since Dec. 29, so you see there is a nigar in the fence some where.

I hope before this reaches you that Cora will be well.

There is no news at this end of the line. I have got some large fine hand made paper and have made one drawing of the *Monaduck* as she is 1000 yards out from quarters. I took it over and showed it to Harvy and he and Getch went wild over it. I am going to draw some of our quarters also "G"s and the fort and send them home on a stick when I get five or six. If they are of any interest to Fargo people they can be put in a window down town. Every one here wants me to make them one but I have come to the opinion that they will look as good in E.H. Sacket's room as any ones. They are 18" x 24" or 9" x 12" according to importance of scene.

FIGURE 36: U.S. "Monadnock" in Mary Island Dry Dock, California. Strohmeyer and Wyman, Publishers, N.Y.

I have had a bad cold for about a month and one half and it makes things miserable for me. I get it almost cured, when I go on guard and it gets worse.

There is nothing to say so I am going to quit.
As you like it,
Gene.

January 26, 1899
Manila, Philippines

Dear Mother:

Just got ten letters and two bundles of papers. The papers were form you. Letters from you dated Nov. 28–Dec 2 - Dec 4 - Dec 9 - Dec 11.

This is the first sheet of paper out of my Christmas presents. I am very sorry to hear of Cora being so sick and hope by this time she is much better. I hope, and so does Harvey that Aunt will stay until we return. By the looks of things it will be only a short time now before we will see Manila

Bay for the last time. I am sorry Aunt is disappointed because I do not write to her personally. I mean any letters for all at home and can't write to all, every time.

I am glad you answered my questions so well. I always answer your letters before writing anything about myself. I suppose I am a crank but I don't like to write to people who don't answer my letters when they write, and for that reason I have chopped off a great many (Miss Payne - Blanche). Miss Payne can only talk about Church Church Church. Blance writes too often and then it is weather - Mamma (Sacket) and your dear little loving brown haired sister Fred. Jenn Condit writes good letters as does my Minneapolis friend. Mina Amerland writes me a good one some time ago. I don't know that I have any girls to back on but I certainly write most to those who give me most news. I wish to keep all your letters so please write in ink. I am going to commence and send them home to E.H. Sacket and don't want them opened till I get there.

Am very sorry that Nig is dead. I guess after I went away he hadn't so much fight in him and got done up. He was a good old dog and was one of the best friends I every had. I remember what Ernice Hansen said that "Nig was my only friend and the only one I respected." Well if all the friends were like him, we could have more respect for them, and the world would be better off. It will go hard with some of the dogs when I get back. I will try and do a better job than John did.

I was down to headquarters yesterday. I am drawing a map of outpost for Maj. White. I saw the Nurses' room and it made my mouth water. Not a hint of dust or dirt-clean mirror-everything in best of order. I understand she is doing good work at the hospital. I have never met her.

FIGURE 37: The Palace—Headquarters of Maj. Gen. Otis—Manila, Philippine Islands

Net time you see Mrs. Walters tell her that the advice about the packing string will be followed out knowing it comes from me having a good bit of experience in the bay window line.

I am glad there is a house across the way. Hope there will be more round about. By the way, are there any pretty girls. I am glad, but not surprised to hear of the provisions father is laying in.

Now about going home. I don't put much stock in it. There has been too much of these rumors here. However it may be so as we have been here so long. Most of us hope that we may return by New York. It would take two weeks longer but he trip would be so much nicer and then we would have been around the world.

The Filipinos are very quiet again and we are having little or no trouble. However the *Monaduck* is kept here for kind of a persuasion for them to keep on as they have. Aquidauldo has been elected president and on the day of his inauguration they had a gay time. They are like a lot of little children. For a while they are quiet then they burst out in some new place. They seem to thing that Uncle Sam can't take care of them. But I would hate to stand in his way if he takes his war dogs for shepherd dogs.

Sunday Jan. 29, 1899: Just received two letters more from you dated Dec. 20 and Dec. 24. In the first you state that you had not head from me for a long time, but you expected mail from *"Scandia."*

I do think that Minn. People think more of getting their boys home than N.D. people.

You state that Dec. 23 I was enlisted 7 months in army. I don't see how that is when I enlisted May 15th.

Am glad you got letter from me on Dec. 24 for Xmas.

You seem to think I can get to my box while on the trip home. Well now just think of 800 boxes lying around so that one could get something to eat. No. No. Those will go in the hold if they go at all. I am going to have $10 to buy me something when I need it.

A law is now passed compelling a soldier's letter to be signed, endorsed by a commissioned officer. There are thousands of Americans here and they all get the benefit which they ought to pay 5 ½ cents.

I haven't much more to say and will close when I get ready. The Oregon is not here yet but is expected every day.

There all kinds of war vessels coming and going all the time and not a day passed but a salute of some kind is fired. It is funny how circumstances changes things. At home I would have gone twenty miles to hear and see an English ship fire a salute. Here I do not get out of my chair to see the firefly. At home I would race down town to see Co. B drill. Here I did not look out of the window when all of Gen. McArthurs division (=2 brigades, =4 regiments each, 8 regiments = 96 companies = 9000 men) was passing by.

Write soon and I will sooner.
Gene

February 7, 1899
Interior Philippines Island
6 mile Manila

Dear Ones at Home:

Well here we are at last away into the uplands of Luzon Island. Little did I think when I wrote last time that I would so soon have good news.

Saturday evening Feb. 4 I went down to see Bert Grafton at Cap. Moffets quarters in old town. At 7 p.m. heard "Call to Arms" blown and I took a run for the Malate about 1 ½ miles away. It was a hard run but every one was doing the same thing and I forgot how fast I was going. As I went by the quarters of the 14th Reg. and the N.D. boys every one was lined up in the street ready for order. I got up to quarters just in time to go out with the Company.

Now we had been called out more than a dozen times before and it had always proved a fake. So it did this time we stand out till about 8:30 and returned. I was disgusted and said I wasn't going to leave a stitch on me when I went to bed. We often left on shoes, leggins or something so that in case of attack we would be prepared.

FIGURE 38: North Dakota Volunteers quartered in the Old Church at Paete, San Antonio, P.I. Photographed and Published by B. W. Kilburn, Littleton, N. H.

About 10:20 p.m. we were awakened and told to dress quietly and without any lights. I got up and simply slipped on my shoes and pants and coat having on only a gauze shirt before.

We went out into the trenches with 150 rounds of ammunition hearing heavy firing at the north of Manila. As the night wore on the firing grew closer and we were posted on the top of the trenches looking to the south in search of niggers.

FIGURE 39: Expecting a Filipino Attach behind the Cemetery Wall, Pasig, Phil, Is'ds.

The night was cold and we shivered and watched-watched and shivered. About 2:30 the 14th opened up fire directly at our lift and you bet we kept a sharp look out. The volleys by companies that they fired were fearful to hear smashing down through the bamboo cutting it off like weeds. We found out next day that the Filipinos advanced on them making a charge and the 14th simply stayed behind their breastworks and pumped 6 cartridges at a time from their Krag Jorgeson rifles into them and made nigger piles 6 deep. This one engagement lasted from 2:30 a.m. till about 8:00 and if there ever was harder fighting any where I would like to know of it. Early in then morning harder some of our company went back to quarters and got our shirts, socks, leggins, coats, shelter tents, etc. Others made coffee and we warmed up on coffee and hardtack. About 7:30 we were served oat-meal, bread, coffee, and meat, but at 7:45 a.m. the fun commenced and we had to leave our breakfast untouched and feed the niggers on cold lead.

The signal was given by a 3.2 inch gun fired from the fort and we all had some nigger picked out and when the gun was fired the niggers hit the dust. Every gun went off at the same time. We had no sooner fired then pin---g came the balls from the Filipinos who were in front. From then till noon it was one ceaseless fire.

At first everyone kept close to ground but as the time wore on we got used to it and stood on the top of trenches to watch the "Buffalo" which was firing 6" shells into the woods all the way from the fort to Parangel 6 miles away. It was a great but awful sight to see the shells burst and send houses, trees, horses, men, etc. flying 20 feet into the air. They went 9miles crashing through trees and landed in the hills far back from Manila. At 10 a.m. a charge was made and about 6 niggers were captured any amount killed and huts and woods set on fire. Harvey got a fine new Mauzer rifle and ammunition.

After they came back we ate dinner and I found I had fired 86 rounds so replaced shells and filled up to 200 rounds.

During the dinner hour we all had great times telling how many we had killed and how near we had come to getting hit. During the lull news came in of the fighting at the North. The Nebraskans had been surrounded but had not only kept their ground but also formed a large hollow square and kept fighting out and had the niggers running. The Kansas regiment fought out along the beach. The Tennessees (of blood fame at Frisco) have started for the mountains and are going yet chasing niggahs. The officers tried to give them commands and they said "Hy! Dah! Don't yo go given weons no orders weons know how to do dis air niggah fightiin." From that time till this they have gone at a break-neck-speed and the Col. Died of apoplexy trying to follow them. They would jump right down into the Filipino rifle pits and club the neggers to death.

After dinner we formed up in regimental front of skirmish line and went down through the woods to Pasay about 6 miles. Dead bodies were seen everywhere and trees cut, houses destroyed by shells. This was the hardest thing I ever did-getting through the bamboo jungle. I have heard of bamboo jungle but never dreamed that it was 1/1000 part as bad as it is. You can't put your gun barrel through it in many places and it forms a solid wall of the sharpest thorns I ever saw. You can't pull a limb 2" without its catching on another. My hands, face, legs, breast were one fester of sores for two days after and it tore my blue shirt in a dozen places getting through. On this march we met very few Filipinos but took 4 prisoners. At Pasay we assembled in the main street and marched on in a column of fours, the march by a round about way so to get to the water works and surprise the enemy. We got about 2 miles from the place when we saw that soldiers (14th) from the other direction had reached there and were firing the native huts (we fired every empty shack as we went along). So we turned around and returned about down the road and established outposts having marched about 14 miles in the afternoon. So you see we were not slow in finding some nice straw and getting to sleep. I felt like I used to when I used to take header off from the old high wheel and would make my legs black and blue or when I would take a long bicycle trip. I am just getting over it.

FIGURE 40: Fighting line near Pasay—the Trenches and Lookout Guard, Philippine Islands

We had 1 slice of bread and ½ cup of black coffee for supper (best meal I ever had in my life). Next morning we all went out jumping (chicken) and ever since have had chicken galore. About noon we found a horse, soon after a rig, and then a harness. Now we keep shipping rice (unshelled) for him and will not have to do so much push cart work as in the past. We get all the food we can eat now and have bread once a day. I had a teakettle and boiled my chicken about 4 ½ hrs and it was fine. Next one I got some grease and had a fry. Good----well I guess so. Today I found a large chest that will make a good box to put my clothing in and I filled it with rice and sent it back on the cart. Also a good lamp with a students white shade on it. I packed them in the oats.

I sent back a full set of dress for a Filipino woman and will try to send them to you so you can start a dress reform.

Feb. 9: We are still in the same position and do not know how long we will stay here. I will keep writing till I get an envelope and a chance to send this into town.

FIGURE 41: 14th regiment fighting from captured Filipino Trenches in the woods near Pasa[y, P.I.

We have just got news that Senate has ratified Treaty of Peace. We are all glad for with this and the Filipinos settled we think there is a chance to get home quicker. Though I don't care to go while there is a chance to keep "old long tom" hot. The latest joke is that Aquinaldo has declared war against the U.S. and promises protection to every American soldier who surrenders. We don't quite know whether this is bomb proof or not.

FIGURE 42: A Sixth Artillery Gatling Gun driving Insurgents out of the brush, Pasay, P.I.

Feb. 10: about 11 a.m. we moved about ½ mile to right, the 14th taking our place. Our present position is about same as other, much nearer town. We are ½ mile from "G". I went up to see Harvey and got two fine Spanish shells one about 1 ½ inch other 2 ½. These were taken off from Spanish boats by Filipinos on or soon after Aug 13th. They had emptied the powder out of most of them and had used it to fill mauzer shells of which the powder had been spoiled.

We just received mail, got 4 letters from home, 1 from father and 3 from mother.

Quarters, **Feb. 10,** 5 p.m.: It is Capt. Geary now. We were suddenly ordered back to quarter and expect to be ordered out to the north at any moment so I will quit and write later.

Gene

Figure 43: North Dakota Volunteers in Camp at San Antonio, P.I. Photographed and Published by B. W. Kilburn, Littleton, N. H.

FIGURE 44: The Heliograph Station—signaling between land and naval forces—near Pasay, P.I.

February 13, 1899
Pasay, Philippines

Dear Ones at Home:

Just six months ago today that the Americans fought into Manila and now are fighting out. Soon after mailing last letter to you we heard firing down the beach 2 ½ miles so fell in and made a forced march out beyond Pasay throwing out a line of skirmishers and closing in on direction of fire. We saw about 20 Filipinos run but did not fire for fear we would shoot our own.

We were ordered back to Pasay about dusk and have been here ever since quartered n the Spanish Monastery. The trouble all happened by about 20 of the 14th men (out on a skirmish) walking right into an insurgent camp. They retreated in a hurry and the insurgents fired volley after volley but strange to say only two soldiers were wounded.

The 4th Cavalry came up and drove the Filipinos across the river to Paranquee. Yesterday troops kept on arriving and this morning the 6th Artillery arrived with 4 Asto 3" guns, - small on wheels but large guns (the Astors have gone home so their guns are in charge of the 6th). We are now awaiting developments but everyone expects to get a chance to shoot pretty quick.

FIGURE 45: The Sixth Artillery watching the effect of their Shells, Pasay, Philippine Islands

Yesterday a sharpshooter was captured in the act of changing his military clothes for "Amego" clothes. He was captured and eats Uncle Sam's rich now. Two other sharpshooters we made good niggers of-they don't eat rice. I was over to the graves of the Filipino Soldiers killed lately. They re buried in shallow graves 6" deep only partially covered and the dogs are uncovering them so that they stink. It is a bad sight and we are going to cover them up. They are buried in any direction so that you can't tell where the head is.

3 p.m.: At 12:45 we were ordered to move out from Pasay and are again doing guard, or outpost duty, at nearly the same place near San Pedro Macate. They seem to always pick the hottest part of the day to move us. We work more in the heat of the day than we did at Frisco. The marches are hot and dusty and hard on feet. I don't wear my shoes only when compelled to but that means only a short time barefoot as we have to keep ready for Insurgents. My feet are in very good condition now, getting used to it. These uplands are fine and breezy-although I let the water alone.

If it were not for the sight of tropical trees I could easily imagine myself lounging around on the straw from the wheat stack of some thrifty North Dakota farmer located in the woods along the Red River. The wind blows quite fresh and cool.

Bob Thompson has just got his Lieut Straps and we are all proud of him.

FIGURE 46: The 14th Infantry entrenched at Pasay, P.I.

Feb. 14: I am lost-don't know whether it is Sunday or Wednesday-had to ask for the date. Word came this morning the Iloilo has been taken without loss. Don't know how true it is but hope it is. We are in the midst of a constant fusillade of shots. All the time shots can be heard in some direction. There is a heavy battle going on away out over a hill in front of us about 2 miles away. We don't know what it is, suppose it is up at "Pasig" or nearer.

We send out scouts all the time to scour the country for niggers to the crest of the hills. They report lots of chickens, but no niggers.

We dig sweet potatoes for meals the same as you do Irish potatoes in July. Peanuts and bananas are not ripe yet but they can be bought from natives who have orchards bearing fruit at all times. Coconuts are a favorite among the boys.

Feb. 15: I was on outpost duty (1/2 mile from camp) all night and had a fine time watching the stars, hearing the noises of the night, and watching the rays from the powerful searchlights on the boats playing across the heavens and tipping the caps of the far away mountains with light.

The battle I spoke about died away about 8:00 p.m. after a boat had gone up the river and fired a few shots in that direction. There were few things to mar the beauty of the silent watch. The rice fields don't make a very good resting place on account of their roughness. I will stop a little and tell you about these rice farms.

In this upland country the Filipino finds a piece of land that has a gentle slope. He at once begins at the lower end and builds a dike across the field. These dikes are from 6" to one foot in height. He then fills it up to the limit with water thus and just inside of the water line makes another dike. Thus you will see when this field is flooded all is covered by water. He keeps on making dikes at the water limit till he has his whole filed diked and can soak it as long as he likes. While the land has water on it the farmer turns his "water-buffalo" loose in the mud and the sludge it up better than a plow. They seem to love the water-hence their name.

Afterwards the water is drawn off and the field bakes in the sun, making it almost impossible to walk over-let along sleeping on. When the farmer wishes to sow his crop he again floods the land and drills in the rice in the mud. The rice is cut with a small cycle smaller than our creass hook and bound up in small bundles bond with straw. Stacks are then made very neat and solid so as to keep the heavy rains off. It is thrashed out as it is needed. The native takes a boundle places it under his feet and works it every way thereby getting every kernel. He gets more, I think, than our modern thrasher but is slower. This operation simply loosens the kernel in its shell from the straw. To hull it they put it in a bamboo basket with a hole in the bottom for the grain to move through. This basket nests in another that is stationary as they shift the upper one on the rough bamboo of the lower one the rice is hulled but not separated. To separate a native boy about as old as Jerome puts about a quart in a large flatbasket 3 feet in diameter and throws it up and lets it sift out. Thus we have chow-chow rice and white and clean. A funny custom of the natives is to build in a cross at the top of the stack so that the lightening won't strike it.

Rice straw looks exactly like oat straw, the kernels being the same.

We have orders now to be in readiness to move on Paranque. We all have a day's rations in our haversack and are anxious to go.

The cavalry went out early this morning. They looked funny on their little ponies (all you can get here) going along in the gray of morning up over the hills and down into the ravines.

Feb. 16: Well about 7 p.m. last night the firing came nearer and so we were all kept out on post all night. This makes it pretty hard but the excitement helps some. I forgot to tell you the outcome of the cavalry charge. They rode along for about 4 miles without being molested when all at once there were Filipinos on all sides of them firing like hailstone but too high (as usual) to do much harm. The cavalry retreated with very small loss- two men wounded, 3 horses wounded, one horse killed. This morning another skirmish was engaged in by the left of our line.

Feb. 18: We moved back-up to our old camp of Feb. 5. This makes us nearer our outposts. I drew a map for Major White today of the battlefield. I will send home a rough copy of it so you can have a definite thought of our position.

More ammunition is being brought up all the time so we will not be short when the time comes.

Feb. 19, 1899: We have been in the field just two weeks today and I, for one, can say that they have been the two most pleasant weeks of my enlistment. Time passes very quickly and every moment sees something new. Last night every man was on the firing line all night expecting an attack. There is very heavy firing on our left. It has been kept up for four days. I have managed to borrow an envelope so will send this letter in by Tad Foster.

Frank Anders is now Corporal. Will Edwards Sergeant.

Best Wishes to all
Gene

I will send map in another envelope as there is not room here.

February 20, 1899

Dear Ones at Home:

I will keep writing a little bit every day and send when ever I can. I managed to send nine pages yesterday. I will enclose map in this letter.

It will be hard-I suppose to trace up our wondering but commence at Paranaque and follow dashed line keeping track of the Dates marked and you will be able to understand where we have been. Will Edwards has written home that you will have the map and they will be able to see it I suppose.

Remember this is not the map I spoke of making some time ago but a rough sketch in the field.

I will speak of our movements in future letters and you can mark them up on the map.

Got mail from U.S. today. One from Father, one from Mother, bundle of papers.

Mail is going to town so must close.

Gene

February 23, 1899
Quarters, Manila

Dear Ones at Home:

I am in quarters for a few hours this morning so will write a few lines and mail it.

Three from Co. are allowed to go to quarters in the morning and three n afternoon. This way it does not take long to get around the company and we all get a chance to change clothes and get a good wash up.

Last night we further celebrated Washington's birthday be digging more breastworks. We have a full line now and are making drains for the wet season.

The 6th Artillery have 4 masked guns in readiness for the Filipinos. Last night the Filipinos tried to cut us short of rations by setting fire to the Commissary. But this was a larger job than they anticipated for the building is of solid stone-walls-floors-pillars with steel roof and the stores within are very slow burning stuff.

FIGURE 47: Commissary Station, San Fernando, P.I.

One officer and two privates were killed by the Filipinos. This made the boys crazy and they started in and burned every bamboo hut in "Tondo" district and drove the niggers out of town, 150 niggers killed.

It looks good to get back and see the bay and large ships but yet I don't want to stay here for it is too lonesome without the boys.

I haven't much time to write so must close. Only write to keep you from worrying. I don't get time to write to anyone else.

Gene

February 26, 1899
Manila, Philippines

Dear Ones at Home:

Co. B just arrived in the barracks this morning after a very dusty march. We were all glad to get a bath and some clean clothes. We relieve "G" from doing guard duty over the fort and quarters. We expect to be in about a week and then go out again. We all hope there will be a let up on the scrapping till we can get back on the line again.

The *Scandia* arrived on Feb. 24 with the 20th Reg. on and an enormous mail from the States. I got 9 letters-5 from home. Am glad you received Xmas presents in good condition.

You speak of receiving two large silk handkerchiefs like the one Mrs. May gave me but do not state who they were from. Mail is expected again to day. This is the most interesting event of our present lives and is looked forward to with a great deal of interest.

Yesterday Major White and I tramped the whole length of the trenches and paced off the distances for a map. I afterwards made a map showing every turn in trenches and length of each, also degrees of angle. Height of trench every 100 paces. Position of each Co. on the firing line, distance occupied-and strength of men. This goes in with the rest of his report. I like the work and Major White more still. All the boys say they will follow Major White where ever he goes. He ought to be Colonel of the Regiment.

There is no more so I will close.

Gene

February 28, 1899
Washington's Birthday
in the
Philippine Islands

Dear Ones at Home:

Today I am celebrating-not as I used to do by taking my skates and going for a good long skate in the fresh cool air of frosty February, but with my shoes off lying in my shelter tent under a bunch of 300 bamboos. This may not seem much of a celebration to you but it would if you had had your shoes and leggins on since the 4th of Feb. I have been rising all day and my feet begin to feel good.

Things are going along very greatly since we threw up entrenchments. An occasional shot is fired over toward San Pedro Macate. I understand that an Oregon boy was up there this morning looking around and a stray shot hit him in the mouth and went out the ear.

March 1, 1899
Manila, Philippines

Dear Mammey:

I finished up 36 hours of guard duty this morning and so went down town to see the burned districts. The one in Tondo where the Commissary was located was about as large as the 4th Ward in Fargo and the one in Binanalo was three times as large as the Fargo fire. In Tonda some fine buildings were destroyed but in Binando they were most all bamboo huts. Every thing was burned up stick and clean and would make a splendid parade ground. It is 5 miles from Malate Districts.

I sent a letter off a few days ago and so there is not much news but as there is a boat leaving tomorrow at noon, I thought I would be sure and have a letter on it.

The 20th Reg's are in and we are hoping that more will be in soon as the work is too hard now and as the hot season is coming on more and more will begin to tell on the boys.

I will close now. Give my best wishes to Aunt and Keep her on ice till we come-when I don't know-I guess May 15, 1900.

Gene

March 6, 1899
Manila, Philippines

The *Ohio* came in last night and I got 3 letters 1 from mother, 1 from Blanche, 1 from Dallas-Jerome-Mrs. W.C. and 3 outside letters. No papers.

We are just preparing to go to the ranches again, being relieved here by Co. D. We are all glad for there is quite a bit of firing on our end of the line and we are missing it all. You must not think that this means more danger for out there we are behind breastworks while, here there is liable to be an outbreak at any moment and we have no protection.

On the firing line **March 7**: We got marching orders yesterday before I had time t finish my letter and so will add more till we get a chance to send mail in.

We are back at our old place on the line and are happy. There is a great deal of firing now and the whistles of bullets is a common sound.

I was on guard last night and about 10 p.m. a bamboo fire started out in front of us and to the right. Immediately there was quite a shots fired both by the insurgents and Americans. It was fun hearing the bullets whistling over our heads and trying to guess whether they were 20 or 100 feet over us, to the right or left. When a bullet comes within 10 ft. there is a peculiar swish or tearing noise such as a nail makes when it buzes through the air after Father would strike it one good blow with his hammer and it would glance (which he doesn't often do). Other wise there is simply an air brake like whistling and you can't tell where it is. So you see when you hear it whistle there is no use of dodging as there is no danger and when you hear it buzz there is no use dodging for it is too late and if it is going to hit, it will long before you can dodge.

The only thing to do is to keep low and well covered.

The out post was about 225 yards from the breastworks and our orders were to shoot if we saw any one prowling around and then get close to the ground and watch for results (well they didn't have to tell us to get down). It there were more than two to fire and run for the breastwork and if there was much firing to come back so we "comed" back and for once in my life I wished I was a "shortey." As it was I made quite a few graceful bows to the bullets as they came over. When we got back the firing let up afor a while and as we thought-for good, but as we again went out a few shots were fired again. We were finally relieved and got in some good sleep.

This morning a white flag appeared about 1000 yards out in front. Major White and interpreter took white flag and went out and waited for them to come out. Presently they came out 100 yards nearer and as they failed to get closer Major White got tired and came back.

In the afternoon the same thing was repeated and they got within about 400 yards of each other when low the bastards opened fire on our officers. If they had known anything about a rifle they would have shot the officers but as it was our officers came back and we all made dust fly around the niggers that had proven themselves such friends. I fired 11 shots at 900 years and took good deliberate aim watching where my bullets landed. The last 3 got pretty close to the niggers. We were all mad enough to kill every nigger on the island without mercy.

Feb. 14: It has been raining pretty steady for the last few days and instead of writing I have been busy building a house to live in. Frank Anders and I are together and have the best "cosa" in the row.

Night before last I was on guard at Headquarters of Reg't and heard all the talk about the attacks on the Filipinos next morning. I awoke the staff at 4:30 a.m. and flew my kite back to Co. B to get my breakfast. Before the sun came up the Cavalry mounted on great nice cavalry horses (brought over on the *Tacoma*) came galloping to the front.

They all went out over the trenches and over the hills to Pasiq (see map). We did not get into the fight and are still in the same place. The noise of the great guns firing up the Pasiq was terrible to hear and all day it kept up only getting farther away. They have no worked away down the big lake.

Other troops have been placed down south of Paranaque (see map) and soon we will have them cooped up in a hollow square.
During the night between 4 and 5 thousand regular infantry were placed on the line.

In this way we will advance and unarm them and then off for Mololos then home.

March 22, 1899
San Pedro Macati
Philippines

Dear Ones at Home:

We have been moved form Overshine's Brigade into King's and are now at the Pedro Macati. Co. B is at the large stone church. I am writing this letter as Gen. King's headquarters. I am on special duty for a few days making sketches of the country for the General. I am now making a map very much the same as the one I sent you but larger and better work and every thing put on. Tomorrow I will go up river and get things more correct. I don't know how long this will last but expect to get back with Co. before long.

I got a letter from Mother stating that father would send one by Hong Kong but I have not received that one yet. Mother's letter told about news of battle.

That telegram to *Forum* was form B not from Col. Trueman.

I got my Geometry from Frank Kneir and am very happy. I have gone 40 pages already.

Must close and get at map.

Gene

April 3, 1899
San Pedro Macati

Dear Ones at Home:

Haven't written for quite a while as the duty keeps us working or sleeping all the time. Two mails have reached us since coming here. I got *Forums* up to Feb. 18. Malolos has been taken but the insurgents have retreated not been taken. Our first blood was spilled pretty freely day before yesterday. Twelve men in each company have Drag Spensor rifles now and these men went out to hunt the enemy.

The fight was one of the latest that has happened so far. Lt. Baldion will have to have his leg amputated probably caused by the bone being shattered. Corporal Byron of D will probably die. Shot through the back at the shoulder ball passing down and cutting spine paralyzing body. Bugler Morgan of D was hit in the head not seriously. Co. D got badly cut up caused by 1st Sergeant trying to call roll in Co. front in field. None of Co. B boys ere in scrape but we were close by so that we saw it all. We have been compelled to move from quarters in town as the Spaniard wanted $400 Mex while the U.S. would only pay $200. Our things are packed up in officer's quarters. I sent a large roll of drawings home. Do not try to flatten them by rolling but place them in big book of mine and leave them for a while so as not to spot the paper. After they are straight take good care of them but let anybody see them who wants to. Map form Escotta to Maliute Fort is not finished. Others can be placed in store window if any one wants to. Fry H. Amerland.

Figure 48: The Insurgent House of Congress on Fire Matolos, P.I. Photographed and Published by B. W. Kilburn, Littleton, N. H.

I intend to frame the picture of Monade [?][?] and our quarters. Save everything except stick and string. I will send a map I bought in this letter.

Gene

I have sent 3 packages papers letters.

April 9, 1899
San Pedro Macati
Philippines

Dear Father and Mother:

News came yesterday to be ready to move in 36 hours so we have hustled everything that we don't really need back to quarters. I have had my drawing board, square, compass, paper etc., etc., out here for the last few days working no a small cottage for you. In case you sell I think it would be just about what you want and if you don't sell Father may use it on some other poor innocent sucker who wishes to build. I have received some very high compliments from the boys here as to its cozy appearances. Major White (who was an old Civil Engineer) thinks it a jewel. Col. Trueman got quite stuck on it-probably because it was not a Filipino hut) and wants me-sometime-to draw up a sketch of a larger house for him. Maj. Dr. Pease has had me draw one for him.

I have not had time to finish but two elevations and one small floor plan. I wish that Father whenever he gets time would try and figure out cost and send me back drawings and bill of lumber, carpenter work, mason work, etc., etc. and method of getting same if it would not be too much work. I want to learn how to estimate. Now I suppose Joe will be so tired that he can't get time to write all this fool trash. If its too much work don't. But there are so many moments in which I could just as well be learning something that will be good to me when I get back. Description of house: Studding 12 ft. -2x4- except nook and porch. The cornice must be lowered. Height of ceiling 8'-6" or 9"-better 9"-but if upstairs is to be used 8'-6" or less would do. I don't figure on finishing of second story, but use it as a store room. However two good rooms could be made here, with low ceilings on each side-to be used in case the prodigal son returns. Foundation-could be of brick or same as old house if put in as good. The steel brick would look very good. A very pretty effect would be made by using stone-or imitation of stone from ground up to window sills around the "nook" or tower. This would break the lines and the line of water-table would not be so menotenous.

Basement: In case a basement or cellar it be put in I would suggest that it be under dining room-bed room and bath room-or simply under dining room. You will notice that I have made no allowance for a stairway into cellar. However, the stairs to second floor could be reversed so as to go from dining room and the way to cellar be in same place as stairs to second floor are now. This would deprive the bedroom of small closet but I think the bathroom would afford changing space for gowns.

Plumbing and electric work-by all means never build another house without good provisions for the bath. I have placed the bath near kitchen so that water may be heated by stove in kitchen. You have a water front on the kitchen stove and the extra expense of a hot water tank would repay you a thousand times in the course of a few years. Put in a regular bathtub whether you have water works or not-or sewer- for if there is anything that is unpleasant it is to trot down cellar for an old musty wash tub. A cess pool could easily be fixed out side of house for waste.

In order to make room for stove and hot water tank on side of kitchen next to bath tub it would be well to shift back door over to where back kitchen window is and visa versa.

In case of cheap lights in Fargo or any place that you would build, it would be a nice thing to have wiring in house all ready for it. This would not cost much, there being no fixtures-only wires. This of course would be a luxury and could be omitted-but you know—you know.

The cistern would not come under plumbing but should come under the kitchen so as to be where it would be direct for pump.

Heating-You will notice that every room I the house-except back bedroom-is in direct connection with a chimney flue. It would be nice to have the back flue run to the cellar bottom to that a heating plant could be put in at any time. The fireplace in parlor would be a pleasant arrangement. It should be built of Philadelphia fire Brick and an ornimental quarter sawed oak mantle. I am just thinking that I could just spin yarns to perfection about the way out in the Filippines in the 90s if I could sit in the growing shades of the evening tide before the glowing throat of a fireplace

> And in the fiercness of the wintry blast,
> When in the home-circle I'd be at last,
> I could say to the North-wind-
> With joyous irth-
> As gathered wid be fefore the
> old home hearth,
> Blow High! Blow Low!
> Not all thy snow
> can quench the life of this ruddy glow.

The tops of the chimneys should be f red pressed brick.

Inside Finish: I think that there could not be any finish as nice as Antique Oak for dining room, parlor, vestibule, and nook. A seat, built in one end of vestibule with lifting cover would make a nice place for rubbers and then "Gene wouldn't have to say "Where are my rubbers?!!!!!??!? I think a finish something like this sketch would be fine. Finishing windows with panel of oak below much the same as our old house. The fluted casing part way up makes a nice appearance with or without wainscoting. The nook would be a fine place for flowers or to pick your teeth after dinner. If used as a lounging place the seat should be finished with green or "pepper & salt" corduroy cushions. There would be an arch between this and the dining room with grille or tapestry hangings.

I have made the dining room especially long so that the table may be at one end and the room thereby make a pleasant sitting room.

All the rooms are larger than found in the average house of this kind yet not too large.

There is a large plate glass window in both dining room and parlor. The upper light of these as well as of the four windows in the "nook" are divided off into small diagonal chinks which set off the cottage to great effect. The same thing should be in door and gable windows.

I need not speak of pantry----Father "saveys mucha."

The kitchen should be wainscoted and painted alight buff, both for pleasantness and dirt. One bedroom would look nice in straw color and the spare room in Sky blue. If oak is not used the parlor would look fine in Ivory White rubbed down to a dull gloss. The dining room would stand more rough and tumble in warm brown.

Finish plastering in rough and "tint" the rooms to suit painting instead of papering which is of short duration, shabby looking after a short time, and is the greatest germ ketcher in the house.

Outside finish: I have thought that narrow 3" siding would be the nicest mitered at the corners. Yet I know of Father's objections to mitered corners and if corner boards are used the wider siding would look better. I have made a belt around the house at the head casing of the windows using up and down (beaded) ceiling or shingles put on thus or thus above the belt, thereby breaking the high look.

At the corners or cut offs on the dining room and parlor gables the frieze runs around on cut offs while the Plancher Facier and crown moldings make a square gable supported by flat brackets width of frieze.

The gables are finished in shingles flush with crown moldings and rounded in the gable windows on original line of studding.

Back of "nook" tower there should be worked in a small tin deck so that snow wouldn't play havoc.

The porch has a fancy post with 1 ¼" square plain oak slats in railing. Some small grillwork above would look good.

Painting:
- siding - pleasant light green
- beaded ceiling - bottle green
- trimmings - dark green
- roof - black

Or if you don't like this
- body - light-medium buff
- beaded ceiling - dark buff
- trimmings - brown
- roof - Baxters English Shingle stain
- Lattice work under porch - light green, grass green

Now I suppose you think I am crazy to describe such a house well I am crazy to see a good American house again.

The 12 Regiment have been out on our line but have gone back. We expect to go to the Luneta this afternoon and sleep there tonight and move on tomorrow.

All letters written to me addressed at Manila will reach me.

We have just heard that as soon as possible the Vols. Are to go home but we suppose that this "soon as possible" means about May 1900.

Frank Andrs got back with all the rest from up the lake and has gone over to Gavite to see Chris who is in the Marines. They are soldiers just like us only travel with the war ships and under direction of the Navy Department.

I don't remember of saying we have three Chinese cooks who get up some great meals.

Co. G is only about 100 yards from us and we do guard and outpost together. I see Harvey a great deal and are very friendly. He cuts a great figure going around in his brown overalls and undershirt. He is well liked by the boys but Getchell is the favorite of both Companies.

Tad Foster has taken examination for Lt. He had use of my Geometry but says the Exam was a sticker. I think however he will go through with flying colors.

Don't get mad at long winded letter.
Write often and much
Gene

April 9, 1899
San Pedro Macati

Dear Ones at Home:

I forgot to put in the maps in my last letter so will send one to you and one to Mr. Amerland direct. I put some Frisco cuts in this letter - save them for me.

The map you now have is more accurate (as much as there is of it) than this one but this one gives you a general idea of the country north of Manila. Just received mail from U.S. last night. One from father, one from mother, Blanche, Albrant. I have been into town on detail and sent home drawings etc. Save everything but stick and string.

I cleaned out my trunk and burned all my letters and other trash. We are expecting to move up on the lake tomorrow but don't know anything about it. It has been reported every day that we were going to move.

Have been in the field now over two months and am not sick of it yet. Would like this kind of service for rest of two years.

Major Pease just tells me that our injured men are getting along as fine as silk. There are comparatively few sick now as we are used to the ran and heat 105°. Send me one more pair of show strings in bundle of papers. They are good and strong and can not be bought here.

We are near the subsistence store here and can get all kinds of eatibles cheaper then you. Sugar 4 cents per lb. (one lb or more at a time), Bartlet Pears 17 cents, corn 10 cents, deviled ham 8 cents, honey 25 cents large bottle. U.S. buys it in large quantities bringing it over in transports and not charging for anything but first cost.

Frank Anders has been picked out with 4 other men of the Co. as scout and left this afternoon for the lake under Lt. Grischus of H who is an old cowboy.

Frank is a fine show and acts as chief of scouts (Corporal).

Every regiment is sending 1 battalion besides scouts and we think a big battle is at hand. I sent package of papers.

Gene.

April 17, 1899
San Pedro Macati

Dear Ones at Home:

"April showers bring forth May flowers" - but not here. April hot days develop sun-stroke. Every day sees it a little warmer and country dryer.

North Dakota's are no rookies (as the regulars call new soldiers) now. I believe the last letter I wrote the boys were loading into scows to be towed up the river, across the lake, and on to Santa Craz. The town has been taken and five of the N.D. scouts have been killed while advancing on the enemy. I suppose you know more than we do about it. The bodies were placed on a boat to be brought down river and buried at Paco but the boat got stuck on the sand bar at the head of the river for about 18 hours through the heat of the day and when the bodies reached the hospital they were rotten and the faces were one swollen mass so that they could not tell one from another. They had to throw them into a box and bury them.

Sergt Maj. Wittaker is dead. Was in the hospital only a few days and died of dysentery. He was one of the best boys in the Regt. And I miss him as we used to have great times taking pictures and making jim cakes. If he had anything he would generally hunt me up to let me enjoy part. We slept together for about a month in the field

I was in town the day of his funeral and they fired salutes over his and three other soldiers all at once. Many are buried without a salute because all the forces are busy on the front.

I stopped the *American* because it cost too much-came too irregularly and never tells the truth about the fights. Will buy a paper once in a while and send home.

I had my picture taken the other day while in town and if it is good will send home some small size $3.00 Mex #12.

I was in the hospital and saw a few of the boys who were wounded. Poor fellows don't think of their pain but beg to get back to fight again.

There are a great many hospital nurses here now and it does one good to see a Red Cross nurse tending the sick fellows with her plain blue dress and pretty white cap and her thousand and one ways about her that a man never masters.

There are all kinds of American ladies here now while back in December there were not enough to make an old hen party.

Co. B has three Chinamen for cooks now and the grubs is better and lasts longer. We all tumble over each other to see what's next for dinner now.

I can't think of anything more now so.
Good By
Gene.

April 20, 1899
Manila, Philippines

Dear Ones at Home:

We are back in Manila today. Came in last night. We were inspected this morning as to shoes, clothes, and arms. We expect to have a physical exam this afternoon.

We are all tired and would like a few days rest but we are expecting orders every moment to go out again-probably to Malolos by train and on up country by hoof-back-this evening. We all want to go if there is to be any fun.

Co. G as usual is next to us. All No. Dat. Is in the Bamboo Barracks now. The agents of our old quarters wanted $400 Mex per mouth and Uncle Sam said "Nit."

FIGURE 49: Reinforcements going to the front, P.I.

This morning about 14 large and small steamers came in and we suppose they are the new Government launches built for the U.S. at Hong Kong.

We hope that there will be some mail as it has been quite a while since we have had any.

It seems quit a treat to be in town again and stare like phools every time a lady goes by.

I got a "Oregon" hat band from Chirs Anders and will send it home in this letter.

I just got a proof of my pictures and will enclose it hoping that it will reach home before fading. Will send others as soon as get them.

Good By
Gene

May 1, 1899[8]
Dear Folks at Home:

Manila, May 28, - To The Forum.
Co. B came in from San Pedro on the south line the night of April 19. We got a very good night's rest on our cots in the barracks, and on April 20 stood inspection by Major Stars. He was quite particular that our shoes and clothing be in perfect order.

---

8   This letter was printed in **THE FARGO FORUM AND WEEKLY REPUBLICAN**, JULY 28, 1899 under the article title " MORE DETAILS: Gene Sackett of Co. B, Writes a Detailed Account of the March of the Dakotans With Lawton. The following report of the march of the North Dakota battalions with General Lawton, was written by Private Eugene H. Sackett of Co. B, who kept a daily dairy."

Letters From Manila—Inland Campaign

STAURDAY, APRIL 22

First call at 3:30 a.m. Good breakfast. Started out on Novaliches road at 4:40. Passed blockhouse NO. 3 before daylight. Off to our left we could see the dim outlines of Le Lame Church (Blockhouse

No. 2). A little farther out we found the camp of the Fourth infantry-as still as death. As we went by we awoke the bugler, who set up in bed and blew first call. We had an hour or so the better of him, and gave him the laugh.

We soon got into a fine country, with gentle hills and great, fine groves. As we progressed the ground grew constantly rought, so that by the time we were to Noveliches we were right int he midst of the foothills.

The Noveliches Skirmish - We met no resistance until we got about nine miles out from town. We then drew a few shots from a Filipino outpost. We could not see them; but we could certainly hear them, and carried ourselves accordingly. The fire seemed to come from the right, but it is hard to tell from which direction a Mauser comes. It makes a small "pop" - "swish" - and that's all. It may be 200 yards or 800 yards to the front - right or left - you don't know. There is no smoke.

H and B were thrown out to the right of the road, in line of skirmishers. The line extended over very rough ground, and for lack of a bugler, the line was poorly kept, as the voice of the captain was not loud enough to be clearly understood on the extreme right or left.

Johny Gearey was sick in quarters and Luther was one of the scouts, so we had no bugler. We went at double time over the hills and rice paddies and did not stop for anything pushing on through brambles and tangled grass, all the time keeping a close watch out for the enemy. However, it is seldom that one gets a chance to see the Filipinos in open skirmish line, as they always chose ground which offers a protection to them. After getting nearly played out we went back to the road and were moved forward again, in column of fours, up the road, almost to the town of Novaliches. Here again we were marched in skirmish line to the left of the road through a very dense growth of small trees. The ground was covered with one tangle of vines, which triped us up and were the cause of many a bayonet being left there. I think that bayonets will be growing there in years to come.

Just as we got out of these trees and in sight of the creek, Corporal Hansche was shot. He had all kinds of nerve and did not seem to care half so mush about the pain. He thought he was shot in the left side, just above the hip bone and kept his left hand pressed on the spot.

Spaulding and I were left to care for him and get him back through the woods to the road and help.

This was a difficult task, as the trees were too close to allow all three to pass abreast. I dropped behind with the guns and accoutrements while Spaulding got Fred through the brush, at a rapid rate. When we got out on the road Lieutenant Putnam, who was lately made lieutenant with Tad Foster, cut the shirt off from Fred. Great was our surprise to find the wound up on right breast just below nipple. The shot was a Mauser and went clear through and out back without striking a slate. The wound was dressed and he was taken back to the ambulance.

There were about a dozen other boys lying in the ditch at this place, prostrated from the excessive heat, and lack of water.

Our force was made up of four troops Fourth Cavalry (old on island)-three guns of Sixth Artillery with their complement of men (old on island) - eight companies of North Dakota (old on island)- eight companies of Twentysecond regulars (new on island). The North Dakotans were in lead and had all of the fighting and hard work of flanking so the average of sick would naturally be high, but by far the greatest numbers fell ou of the two new regiments - Twenty second and Third.

General Lawton was in the road with his staff when we got back with Fred. He is a great big man about the build of Dr. Vidal, only taller. He has a look on him that means business. He was mounted on a great American horse, any of which look large in this country of pickanninies. He wears a great high helmet and Mausers fly thick wherever he goes, but he never gets punctured, which, with all the big target he makes, goes to prove the poor marksmanship of the Natives.

I did not get a chance to fire a shot that day as so many of the company did. I missed the plunge in the creek which all the boys declared "great." The boys have not got done wondering how they all got over that creek safe.

Captain Gearey was the first to take to the "aqua" and he went in out of sight at the first step, only his hat being visible on top. He had his full outfit on besides the outfit of one of the boys who had fell out.

Quite a few guns were dropped in the creek while the boys were trying to get over but were afterwards recovered.

When the boys got to the top of the hill, they let a yell out of them, and though most of them say they didn't have breath enough to move a feather, it made the "insurectas" move "pronto."

A general halt was ordered to give the bull teams time to get over the creek, which had to be forded. We were glad to get our rounds of hardtack and jassack. During the afternoon we rested up-swapped lies-and all tried to tell, just how deep that creek was. I was pretty tired and instead of taking in the park, water works, town hall and operahouse I washed my feet.

SUNDAY, ARIL 23

Had breakfast before sun up, but as North Dakotans were to be rear guard for the day did not get started before 10:30. It was very slow work with the long line of bull carts and we were doomed to have day after day of the most tiresome work, getting those teams over hills and through ravines. A "Veeder" cyclometer would be insufficient to register the number of hills and a 180 degree protractore their steepness.

After two days of making a regiment take care of the train for a day, they changed and made every regiment take care of their own carts. This was much better, as it equalized things up a good bit. Then more men could be detailed on each cart.

The foothills commence at Noveliches and we only get about two and half miles during the day. We camped near water and every company went out around the camp and did guard duty. The Twenty-second were in advance during the day and were about five miles ahead of us. They carry two days' rations in their haversacks and so do not have any mess wagon.

Figure 50: Resting by the way, Lawton's expedition, P.I. Photographed and Published by B. W. Kilburn, Littleton, N. H.

A marked difference was noticed between the old and new troops. The former carried as little as possible, many having no pouches or dishes. The latter were under orders to carry certain articles and were threatened a court-martial, if they left anything behind.

They started out from Manila with shelter tents, tent poles and pegs (in a bamboo country) pouches, big government blankets, extra woolen underwear and shoes. I hefted one blanket roll, that must certainly have weighed eighteen or twenty ponds. This was the cause of so many of their number dropping out, exhausted. About the second day out from Novaliches you could see their trail by the blue blankets, pegs, pins, etc., scattered over the field. Better to stand court-martial then chance getting planted in the Filipines. For a few days the Twenty-second men carried the blanket for a ways in the day time, and when night came the crafty North Dakota boys would go out and get it to sleep on, leaving it in the morning for next lucky man. So you see we were all glad the Twenty-second carried blankets.

I knew one happy-go-lucky fellow in our regiment, who started awa from quarters with only a canteen. When meal time came, a tomato or meat can was produced for coffee and he evidently believed in the old adage "fingers were made before forks." At night he would get straw or something else to cover him up and next morning be as fresh as the rest of us.

When we first got into the hills, we did not know what was before us and all kinds of reports were circulated about two more hills and then a good road. But the two hills were multiplied and squared and raised to the ninth power until finally we began to think they were very much in the plus quantity and we in the minus. Every one was steeper, rougher, higher and harder to get those carts over, then the one before.

Quartermaster Sergeant Palmer and Joe Schlanser would drive on ahead to get us some hot coffee. Then they would have to "hike" all over to find the company again. Some times we would have the pleasure of being marched past the good smelling life giving hot coffee, and not be halted until quite a distance beyond. In a short time, however, up would come the "Chinos" with the coffee boiler on a stick between them.

Ernie Plamer is a hustler and see that Co. B gets every thing that's going. Joe, as you know, takes interest in anything he touches and things have a snap to them when he is around. His little team of cabellos go through the worst without "changing cars."

In the afternoon we got on top of a great hill, which was a kind of a hogback, between the mountains and the sea. Before us, at our feet, and reaching away up to the mountains was a wild rolling country, dolled here and there, with clumps of trees. At last we had reached a country where water was abundant, cool and sparkling form a thousand springs. Behind us could be seen the gray streak of the bay. We thought that the climbing was through with but it was only just commenced. Soon after the bull on one of our carts (we had two to each company) died, and we were obliged to pull it ourselves for the rest of the day. We were "Bully Boys." About 7 p.m. another bull was gotten and so we were relieved. With Walker-an old teamster of early days-as our engineer and fireman of the cart things went along fine. We reached camp about 8:30 and each company took up quarters in its respective square at Hotel de Rice Paddy, key to room office.

MONDAY, APRIL 24
Got a good start, but before long found a hill and so kept pushing and shoving until we got into San Jose late that night.

This has been an important old town one day, but houses have long since been destroyed and only the ruins of the old church are left now. The Spanish troops met a heavy loss at the hand of the insurgents some time in '96 here.

TUESDAY, APRIL 25
We resumed our upward course on the straight and narrow way with as much zeal as any Sunday school boy, and at 4 p.m. we received our reward. We were in sight of the promised land, flowing with sugar and

mangos. We were on the highest hill yet reached, and on all sides of us was a sight well worth the hard work of the few days previous. We were only on a foothill, but it was like a mountain. Back of us lay the rolling hills, we so dearly remembered, and to our left, about twenty-five miles, as plain as though it were only five, was the bay. Corregidor Island, Manila, Malolos, and the China Sea.

Then, in the other direct - I can't describe it. It was too grand to take in all in one look. Nothing I have ever seen before equaled it. Just below us, I should say about 1,000 feet, lay a land-locked valley, its breadth reaching away five miles or more to the very foot of the great mountains. In length it reached as far as the eye could see. Down through the center of this beautiful valley ran a crystal-white mountain stream, which weved in and out like a silvery ribbon. On each side, intricale, and as pretty as any senora's lace mentille were the thousands of rice paddies.

FIGURE 51: Interior of Santa Ana Church—our field Hospital during the fight—Philippines

Away up in the mountains a fierce storm was raging, while all was sunshine around us.

From the top of this hill we have the world by the tail, and down the hill. Everybody is happy, and things move along at a brisk pace.

Norzagaray lay about a mile to our right, and as we came down the road we saw two soldiers running out to meet us. Thus it was evident that Hale's division, consisting of parts of the Minnesotas, Oregons, Fourth Cavalry and Utah artillery, had reached the valley before us. We found that they ahd taken and burned Norzagaray and Angat.

We pushed on the Angat for supper and the night. We got into our rice paddies about dusk and had just commenced supper when the rain began to pour down in good shape.

I had luckily procured a rude covering and some dry straw before the rain came, so I was nice and dry all night. After the rain was over, the water lay about two inches on the level, and the boys had a great time fishing their shoes, socks, blankets, etc. out of the swim. All joined in singing "Through out the Life Line." "Cleansing Wave," "Send the Light," and others. Charley Nord said, "I wish I were in my father's barn, I would be near the house," Soon another fire was started and the supper was all the better for the soaking. After supper, fires were started, at which the wet clothes and blankets were dried.

Next morning we all made a scoot for the river, which we had seen the day before. It was clear, swift and cold, knee deep, and stone bottom. We had a good rest at Angat, while supplies were being brought up from the railroad.

The second day I was out on outpost on the top of a high hill, from which a good view of the country could be seen. General Lawton came up three times during the day-always in shirtsleeves. In the afternoon he and the Chief Scout Young came up and watched the smoke for a battle taking place up in the mountains between Hale's brigade and the enemy. They went down and soon after we saw Young, with two North Dakota boys, fording the river. They did not get far before the insurgents fired on them.

Young was not long in locating their hiding place, and soon dislodged them, with his trusty rifle. As they ran off across the open, now and then, one would drop showing that Young was still at them.

After the rations came up we set on down river with Hale's brigade on opposite side. About five miles down we ran into the insurgents, who sent the bullets our way, a little close to our heads. We were at a standstill and they sounded closer. We all ducked. I noticed a regular army major get down behind 3 banana trees-about as good as so many weeds. When we got the order for "Forward" one of the boys whom we call "Major," did not hear and his rear rank man said, "Come! Come! Major, this is no time to be hanging back." The old army major straightened up to his full height, looked with a great deal meaning and walked away. The North Dakota regiment was swung around to the left to cut the enemy on the flank, but they got away too quick. One place they had some beautiful shots at us, and used the advantage. Charley Pepkie of Co. I was wounded, Ed Peterson of Co. B got a Mauser in the heel of his shoe. Ed says: "The Bullet flew and went right through my shoe, my shoe, etc."

FIGURE 52: Filipino Buffaloes—hauling Water to the Front—San Pedro Macati, Philippines.

After a hard march over the hills we came back to the road, tired and exhausted. We were cheered by having a message read to us, that Corporal

Hanche was improving fast. We ate a hearty meal of beef and tacks, expecting to go on in the afternoon, but General Lawton got a message from Manila instructing him not to leave Angat, that hostilities had ceased for a few days for the insurgents to surrender. But they didn't surrender and so after the allotted time had expired we went forth form Angat again on our way down the river to Balinag. Some fightng was done, but the natives have no stick to them. We camped one night in Bustos and then went over the river to Balinag, only twelve and a half miles from the railroad. We had to take off our clothing to ford the river and some snapshots were taken while the boys were in the water. The boys had a song: "From Bustos to Balinag is just one mile. And from Balinag to Bustos is just one Mile." Forty-nine verses-all the same.

FIGURE 53: On the march

The plazo which is a feature of every Spanish town, was soon filled with Uncle Sam's teams, full of supplies for the ever-hungry soldier boy.

The church and the market are the center of gravity in Balinag. The church is modern and looks nice. The chaplain of the Twenty-second held Catholic services there on Sunday, and had an interpreter for the natives.

At the market place mangos are the principal thing sold. They taste much like a peach, in Manila they are expensive ranging from 10 to 20 cents.

Here they cost 2 cents (Mexican) and were fine. Mike Nelson, one of the best-natured men in the Company, had a great appetite for these mangos. He is no called "Mango Mike from Balinag." He has a husky "bolo gang," who are always ready to remember the *Maine*.

Aguinaldo had stored over 10,000 bushels of rice in one storehouse at Balinag, which he had taken from the natives as a war tax. This was all given out to the natives again by the American soldiers. And a hard task it was to keep the natives form pushing the gates in. They must have been 5,000 in that swaying mass of humanity.

In leaving Balinag we went directly north for San Miguel. The scouts had taken this town a few days before and the Oregons and Minnesotans were quartered there.

Young was shot inteh knee at San Miguel and afterwards died an agonizing death of lock-jaw. He and his scouts had done a great work, and had saved many a life by their brave and fearless methods of going on ahead of the main army. He always said, "Come on boys, I'm going" and never gave an order all the time he was in command. It was always in the form of a request.

He had the utmost confidence and respect of all his men. We all felt blue when we received work of his death. We passed through San Miguel and rested for a short time just out of town but the orders were for us to hurry up to the Oregons, for we were to be in the lead at the taking of San Isidro. It rained in the afternoon when we were glad to get sleep. We had caught up at last.

At 3:30 a.m. were up and off for the front.

When we got across the river and in view of the town, the North Dakotans were through in a skirmish line to the right and the Twenty-second to the left of the road. The scouts were on ahead drawing fire, while we got positions. We maneuvered around in back of the enemy, and great was their surprise when they found us there. They dropped everything and ran past us only about 800 yards away. We all got some beautiful chances at them, and I think did some good work, judging form wounded and killed left on the ground.

Twenty-seven wounded; five killed.

We progressed in a skirmish line up through the bamboo without seeing any more and finally came out on a street. The Chinos dived into the houses, and soon we were all eating mangos. When it was found that there was nothing more to do we marched into the center of town and had dinner.

In the afternoon I took a stroll around and found quite a few things, one of which I will mention. This was the prison where the insurgents kept the fourteen American Prisoners. I will send you some sketches of it, also map of our trip. The prison had partly been finished by the Spanish before the insurgents had gained the upper hand in the country. Part of the roof had been put on and had it been finished and a sewer to the river been laid, it would have been a very fair prison, but it was simply nasty with filth. The cell in which the Americans had been kept was by far the cleanest, but was not place to stay.

The poor fellows had nothing but poor bamboo beds or benches to sleep on. They were confined in the stocks, which are large wooden planks with rough holes cut through them for the feet. Between two holes on one of these stocks was scratched a checkerboard on which the poor boys made their time pass more pleasantly. One of the prisoners had written a letter and stuck it through the crack in the floor. He directed the finder to look on the stock and see the blood on the under side from a sore that had been worn in his foot. They were whipped, stoned, starved, and made to clean the dirty prison with their hands. Their own cloths were taken from them and China "clouts" given them, and in these were made to go over the road without shoes in the hot sun. Their backs were in blisters and their feet sore.

Here are their names as they were printed on the walls of the prison:

Captured Jan. 27, 1899
    J.O'brien - Prospector
    A. Sonnichsen - U.S. Transport Service
    H.Huber - Hospital Corps

Jan. 30
    W. Bruce - First Nevada Cavalry
    E. Honnyman
    A. Bishop - Battery H, Third Artillery

U.S. Yorktown, Captured April 12, 1899
    Lieutenant Gillmore - U.S.N.
    W. Walton - Chief Quartermaster
    P. Vaudoit - Sailmaker's Mate
    J. Ellsworth - Coxswain
    L.P. Edwards - Landsmen
    S. Brisolese - Ordinary Seaman
    A. Peterson - Apprentice
    F. Anderson - Landsman

From San Isidro we again went down river. This was a beautiful country, and as we marched along we could see mango groves on all sides. When we got in sight of San Anionia we ran up against the enemy again. Our company, however, was doing rear guard duty, and we didn't see any of the fighting. The artillery fire was the heaviest on the trip. A guard was thrown out around the train, and nothing much was done till morning, except a couple of Filipinos shot. One was shot by a sentry of the Twenty-second just at the left of us. The ball went through his head. In the fight of the afternoon before one Twenty-second boy was shot seven times in the legs, and lived.

Figure 54: The prison where the insurgents kept the fourteen American Prisoners. Drawing by Eugene H. Sackett

Next morning we went on down the river to Cabieo, at which place we stayed till the other division caught up to us. We then pulled out and kept on down the river towards the town of Arayat, which receives its name from the mountain near it. This mountain rises abruptly from a level plain to the height of about 3,000 feet, and is a landmark for miles around. It can be seen from Manila when the weather and sun is favorable. In going up to San Isidro the road had so many crooks in it that this mountain seemed to be on all sides of us. The boys said the mountain was on wheels and the Filipinos were trying to hoodoo us.

Before we got to Arayat we had to cross the river, and as it was too deep to ford with the bull-carts, we had a great time getting over. The water was up to our necks-those of us who had high necks. The little man gets the worst of it in the army except when the bullets come his way. We had the pleasure of shaking hands with second Lieutenant Foster at Arayat. He had been sent back from our company at Angat to get his commission, and is now with Co. H of the Ninth.

Co. B was on provost guard that night and it was about midnight before we got to know just what to do, and where to do it.

Next morning we again set out, and it was very evident that they were working us back towards Manila. We passed through St. Ana, then turning to the left, we went over to Candeba. This is the head of navigation on the river up from Calumpit, and the sick were sent down on boats. We were all getting pretty near done up. But only those who couldn't go any farther would give up. Many had worn their shoes out, and all had sore feet. Every one was ragged and dirty. Two-thirds had dysentery or diarrhea, and not a few had rheumatism.

The rains were so heavy that (?) over a day at Candaba. The Oregons got orders to go to Manila and prepare to go on ship for the United States. This made us all feel good, as we thought that the time was not very far distant for our relief.

The Oregons and Minnesotas started for Calumpit together, through the mud. We and the Ninth started next morning, took dinner at St. Lonis and slept in the church at Apalit that night.

This church had recently been repaired up, and the frescoing on the ceilings is a work of art. All of the North Dakotans slept within-and had room to spare.

Next morning we had a short walk into Calumpit. There is a fine steel railroad bridge of three spans over the Rio Grande de Pampanga at this place. The track is well laid, but the rolling stock is poor. It is an English concern. There are not wooden bridges on the entire length of the line-all steel.

After a two day's stay at Calumpit, we took the train-no I mean the train took us-to Manila. We got inside, outside, on the top, and were crowded. Just think! Seven little dumpy coaches-seven dumpy box cars-for the [?] and mules of the battery-all [?] and North Dakotans. And the train wasn't a quarter as long as one of our trains pulling out of Fargo. All this heavy load was pulled by a dumpy Scotch engine-the Scotch are great on the pull-aren't they? We thought the engineer would roll us off the train in his wild rush over a recently relaid track, where insurgents had been using the grade to fillup their trenches, and thus playing havoc with the grade. But we didn't care whether school kept or not, we were going to Manila and were as tickled as though it was home. We had been gone thirty-six days, having covered a distance of 170 miles, and had seen all of the campaigning in the Philippines we wanted to for awhile.

We got to the water front in Manila about 8:30 and only had a short march of about two miles home to quarters-fresh bath and clothing-did our cots. We went through town singing - "Hot Time" - and causing all kind of wonderment at the hands of the quiet, easy going Spaniards. We were happy, and when we came in sight of the bamboo barracks set up a cheer that brought every sick North Dakota boy from his slumbers in the barracks.

The long trip was at an end - the packs thrown off, and pandemonium reigned supreme, till most midnight.

Gene

May 28, 1899
Manila, Philippines

Dear Ones at Home:

Got back from north trip night before last and have been too tired to write. It seems good to get back to town once more. Most everyone is worn out and all the clothing is completely worn out. However the hospital report is very very low, and every one says the boys look good.

I got two ingrowing toe nails on big toes pulled out this morning. It was quite painful for a few moment but will I hope end a great deal of nursing for me. I have a touch of reheumatism but not so bad as it might be. I will write about our travels later on and give you a good account of them.

We started April 21 and got back May 16. Went about 170 miles. Went through 19 important towns and many small ones besides those on the R.R. from Galumpit to Manila. We don't know just where we will go next but it will probably be to Paranaque or stay here.

The Oregons are ordered home so we suppose we won't be more than a year now in getting away.

I got a letter from Miss Templeton and she spoke of you.

I can't think of any more now so good bye.

Gene.

June 2, 1899
Manila, Philippines

Dear Folks:

We are ordered to be ready for the line at any time. We all have long faces and curse the gods. We have not all got well from last time and now to push us out again and leave the regulars here in Manila to get used to things is too much and we think old woman. Otis has it in for us. Evidently he intends that we all shall bo back on the same boat providing he can get small enough boxes for us. The Oregons had their stuff all in the custom house ready to go home when they were ordered out on the line again. They are nearly at point of desertion. We never expect to get home till our service is up.

Frank Anders is very sick in hospital with fever and Chris was over yesterday to see him. We went together but he is too sick to talk to any one. He didn't know us at first but after a time got over his drousiness. The Dr. say he hopes for his recovery. Chris is a great big lad now and good natured as ever.

If I don't write any more for a time don't worry, for I don't know where we will go. Keep writing to me as it gets to me some where at some time.

In haste,
Gene.

June 2, 1899
(letter sent to Eugene)

To
Mr Eugene Sackett

With
Company B, 1st Reg., N. Dakota
Manilla, Philippine Islands

My Dear Friend,
Please receive this sincere and cordial greeting from you teacher and the members of your Sunday School Class, assembled this morning at my home in pleasant re-union to which has been duly left with your Parents to be forwarded to you or retained with until your return.

Our hearts are with you; and may God bless and keep you safely until we meet again in peace. May the days of your further absence be few.
Faithfully yours,
W. G. Taylor

> "We great you, though so far away,
> For memory holds dear
> The boys who left us one sad day
> Our hearts oppressed with fear
> For well we know that some might fall
> And prayed that God would shield
>
> For boys who now, we trust, are safe
> With Lawson in the field.

No night as glass mates we are met
    Our friendships to renew
But in our joy we'll never forget
    Our soldies brave and true.
A youthful quartette left our class
    Their mettle unrevealed.
But gallant record have they made
    With Lawton in the field.

God bless our soldiers one and all
    O be as brave to Him
A s you wee to your country's call,
    Luck glory cannot dim
And when war's lessons have been taught
    By patriot valor sealed
We'll welcome home our boys who fought
    With Lawton in the field."
        W.G.T.

Letters From Manila—
Hospital and Transport Home
June 12, 1899 to September 22, 1899

June 12, 1899
Manila, Philippines

Dear Folks:

As my last letter told you we left Manila for the south line again. I went with the regiment as far as Pasig but was so weak from diarrhea that I had to come back to town. I don't know when the rest will come in but by the way things look they all will be in the same as myself if they give them time and feed them right.

Morong on the lake is where they are located now. They get supplies by boat.

A fierce battle has been going on around Paranaque but I just heard that they had entered the town.

The Oregons are loading on ship today. We hope to go soon but I have studied the arrival of transports pretty thoroughly and can't see any place for us before Aug. some time.

I have sent a 40 page letter in three envelopes (too large for one) and you may have it printed in *Forum* if you like[9]. Most of the boys now in quarters

---

9 See Appendices "The Fargo Forum and Weekly Republican, July 28, 1899 MORE DETAILS" for reprint of letter.

have had it read to them for correction and say it is correct, and very good. Please let me know what you think of it.

Go through it and correct rhumantisim - diarrhoea - dysentery - and others you notice wrong. I will enclose a sketch of prison cell and map of our trips.

Get the letter back from *Forum* and save it for me with sketch and map and I will spin you some good yarns when I get home.

Am weak but better,
Gene
No mail for 15 days
write-write-write
I sent drawing and map in roll.

June 30, 1899
Manila, Philippines

Dear Ones at Home:

I think I informed you in my last letter that I was sick in quarters with dyhorrea. Well on June 19th my head began to ache badly ad I had that stirred feeling all over my body. It continued worse every day till finally I was sent to the 1st Reserve Hospital with "Supposed Typhoid Fever" on my card. I was hardly able to get from quarters down to the hospital. I was assigned to ward No. 10 and was very glad to get to bed and cover up with a blanket for I was taking chills. I was put on liquid diet consisting of milk (good cow's stuff) beef-tea, vegetable soup, chocolate, eggnog and egg omelets with crackers. You can see I didn't starve. There is a lady nurse in each ward and she tended to me in first class shape.

In a few days I was placed on light diet consisting of butter, bread, oatmeal, tapioca, eggs, oysters, tea, etc. This was a little better for a hungry boy.

In the mean time the Dr. told me that I had Malaria and be careful of chills.

Today I was changed from the 1st Reserve Hospital to the 3rd Reserve about 1000 yards east of the Luneta. I just got here and everything is nice and sweet. The hospitals are carried on in much better shape than I thought.

The *Sherman* and *Grant* are both in now and I think we will be on the move by the 15th.

Just got two large packages of magazines from John and am devouring them in great shape. There are also some books which I will save to read on the boat back.

This is the first I have received from him. I got a letter from father and mother which as usual said "come home." Well I will when I get good and ready (as Uncle Sam does).

I don't want you to feel worried over my sickness as I am able now to be about all the time. And it is good I don't have to do duty out on the line during these hard hard rains.

Got a nice intersting letter form both Emma MacLein and May Ruthroff.

The 4th of Juneryears is oon to come off and all the business houses here are decorated for it. There are thousands of dollars being spent on celebration, the first in Manila.

I am writing in a nice clean place at a window where I can look out n a beautiful garden rich with flowers and trees of tropical growth. Out further is the Pace which connects the Luneta and Escolta. Thousands pass along. A little further out is the great wall of Old Manila.

I must close now got bundle of *Forums*.

Gene

July 11, 1899
Manila, Philippines

Dear Mother:

Received your letter of May 26 and 28 just now through the kindness of Tad Foster who was just in to see me. I have not got a good pen so will have to use lead pencil. I am still in the supplementry ward of 3rd Reserve Hospital as it aught to be called but for old Otis who wants to make the officials in the U.S. think there are only two hospitals here. There are nearly 5,000 soldiers sick in hospitals.

I have been getting along nicely but don't feel so well today. The rain makes every thing damp and I caught a slight cold which affected my bowels causing sharp pains (such as caused by water melons or cowcombers-so you see there are advantages in every stage of the game.

The North Dakota regiment are being paid off today but I can't get up there so will have to go and draw my pay when I get well.

While I was sick in quarters I spent quite a good deal for light diet and so am short. I am not going to buy but very little here so I will have an extra mouth full on the way home. There is nothing worth getting here and now since the vols. Have commenced to buy so much before going home- the thieves of natives and chenos have put four prices on ever thing. I have been told you could buy all kinds of mauzer shells in Frisco also anything else. This sounds right from what I saw in Frisco.

You must excuse poor writing for I am weak in the fore-tops.

Tad is looking fine and a boy in the hospital here who is in his Co. says he is one of the finest of the 9th. He seems sorry he can't go home and told me sure to write to him.

Our regiment is in town now relieved from duty and have orders to go aboard the *Grant*. Probably the meat boat will be here before long and she can get those supplys and comissary (grub). This will take about two weeks and I think no more if all goes well. We will go by Nakasaki and not by Honolulu so I will not see Miss Templeton. And if you would also have been disappointed if you had gone there.

Frank Anders is up and around now. He has been a pretty sick boy and came very near to croaking.

A telegram will probably be sent the day we sail so you will know when to chop off sending letters to Manila. But that will get to you before this I expect unless it is another case of "fool."

Gene

July 13, 1899
Manila, Philippines

Dear Father:

I have managed to get a pen for a few minutes and will write you a letter to let you know how much I appreciated that one of yours with the remarks on estimating in it.

You aught to have "Bess" here in the rain if you want her to have a good shower bath. It rains hard every day, every night, every minute-all the time. The amount of rain fall for the twenty four hours ending 6 p.m. July 11 was four and 37/100 inches!! What do you think of that. You need stilts to get around the streets of Manila. The "Pasig" has over flown its low banks. The Maiquina valley is one vast lake and the water from the pumping station is red with mud. The storm signal has been up for 5 days thus preventing any ship from leaving the port. The cause of all this is a heavy typhon in the China Sea moving slowly north towards Japan. We are only getting the edge of it. Probably you remember how I used to nibble the edge off of cookies-same here-edge of typhones are enough for me.

I am feeling some better than when I wrote Mother. Cap. Geary, Liet. Thomson, and Lieut Smith have just been in to see me and left $31.20 which made the visit all the more pleasant to me.

I have got three packages of reading material from John which help a long ways toward passing away the time. I have found that no matter where you go in this world you can find work in your line. This time the surgeon got me to draw a plat of this hospital for the chief surgeon. It was 24" x 30", scale 22' to 1" and looked good considering the ink used-the old door for drafting board-at least it was good enough for them to ask me to draw up a plat of the 1st Reserve-but as that hospital is about 10 times as large as this I couldn't see it that way and so told them my eyes were sore. See the joke? No? Well you will when I tell you that they took my word for "honest igun" and are now trying to find out just what is the matter with my eyes. They have examined me twice and the Dr. said last night that they wanted to look at them again this afternoon. My eyes are better then theirs I should judge by the results of their examination.

Well, for the first time, I can say it looks now as though we would get started for home very soon and I am glad as the saltwater air will be sure to stop the diarrhea. We now have orders to go aboard the *Grant* as soon as ready and again I am glad for she is the largest and finest transport n Uncle Sam's service. I have always had a desire to go some where on big boat and she is 547 feet long. Go to the front gate and look down towards White's and measure with your eye that distance and then think of her being only 53 feet broad. Five decks 200 soldiers, No. D., Idaho, Wyoming, rest of Vol. Reg., no room for poor old 13 Minn. Have to wait for next boat.

I must stop
Gene

August 7, 1899
Christian Endeavor
Seaman's Home
Nagasaki, Japan

Dear Ones at Home:

This is my birthday and I am spending it pleasantly in Nagasaki. This is the cleanest town I was ever in and is a wonder at every turn. I am not feeling very good so keep rather quiet. I will not write much for I have plenty to see.

Gene
We leave here day after tomorrow for Yokohama.

August 30, 1899
Frisco, Cal.

Dear Father and Mother:

Hello from this side of the world. Quite a while since I have posted a letter to you from this place.

I am well but feeling just a bit dumpish after the trip. We had a most enjoyable trip all the way coming by the way of Nagasaki and Yokohama. A most enjoyable time at both places was ours and we have nothing but praises for the good people of America both at home and abroad.

At Yokohama we were in port two days when we were ordered into quarantine for smallpox. The doctors made a mistake in thinking it was smallpox but we got a free scrub and now have the experience of being through the pleasures of quarantine.

It seems as though we have come through a venerable millpond it has been so smooth all the way over. Very few threw up and there has been little increase of sickness on board. Here is a table of mileage from Yokohama to Frisco registered by the boat every noon.

Aug 14 – left Y. at 5 p.m.
Aug 15 – 229 miles
Aug 16 – 287 miles
Aug 17 – 262 miles
Aug 18 – 254 miles
Aug 19 – 278 miles
Aug 20 – 291 miles
Aug 21 – 297 miles
Aug 21 – 289 miles {crossed 180th Meridian making 21st 46 hrs 42 min long.
Aug 22 – 278 miles
Aug 23 – 287 miles
Aug. 24 – 298 miles
Aug 25 – 300 miles
Aug 26 – 297 miles
Aug 27 – 281 miles
Aug 28 – 275 miles
Aug 29 – 104 miles

Figure 55: A Morning Ride in a Jinrikisha, Sugita, Japan Strohmeyer & Wyman, Publishers, New York, N.Y.

The *Grant* is a fine large boat but could be improved a great deal for the service she is in. The main advantages of her over the *Valencia* is tables for all to eat at, and large wash rooms and water closets.

She goes into repair at Frisco this time for she has not had a stop since leaving New York last February.

This letter has been written on the boat and so in order to get it off to you as quick as possible will seal it up and mail it on the boat.

I will write later on one of the postals you gave me when [?] away and which I saved till now.

Gene

August 30, 1899
San Francisco, Cal.

Dear Father and Mother:

We got into harbor last night at 11 p.m. and this morning went through quarantine inspection in about two hours. We are now lying in the stream waiting for the *Waren* to pull out so as to give us room so you see we are not landed yet. "So near yet so far." I got a big batch of letters from home and elsewhere this morning and have taken all my spare moments to read them. This paper and envelop came in a letter from Blanche and as all my envelopes are ruined I am going to use it in writing to you so you will be the first. I have not time yet for others but will soon.

Early this morning tugs filled with people form N.D., Idaho, Wyoming, and other places came off to us with many brass bands playing but they could only play and wait till we passed through quarantine. About 9 we were released and they they came abors. Edgar was among them also Spaulding. He remarked that you were well and had sent on over coat to me. I am glad you were so thoughtful. I have an army overcoat I have had all the time. He remarked that I looked rather poorly but I am weighing 30 lbs more than I did in Manila. I am alright now but my stomach which needs some johny cake and milk from the jersy cow. I am going to try and get milk here in Frisco and come home well.

Three has been a great crowd on board all day and I am very tired after so much excitement.

I had a good American apple to day and it was GOOD!!!

All is hurry and hurry now so I will close so that this will get to you soon. Give my best regards to all.

Gene

September 19, 1899
Frisco, Calif.

Dear Mother:

I will drop you a few lines this morning to let you know that I am good and alive and longing for home and the "Barber pole.'

We will probably start for home one week from today if everything turns out all right. I am having a very pleasant time here with the folks but yet I am longing to be off for home.

This is a great town to get bargains in and I think I will buy a few things before leaving. Shoes, underwear-etc. I found a book store the other day that carries all kinds of Architectural books and I am going to get a few to keep me busy next winter. Drafting instruments are also very reasonable here too.

I have often wondered if there is any job I can get at home that will be mostly inside work or if I will have to stay home with Ma and keep the stove warm.

If I don't get a job I am going to study up at home on house building so that I can be more good when I do get to work.

I did not notice that this paper was torn when I commenced.

Figure 56: Visit to Yokohama, Japan, on the way home.

I am getting stronger and more healthy looking every day under Aunt's care and will look better when I come home than I did when I went aeay.

I should judge by the papers that all Class is going to be at Fargo to meet us. Well let them come. I would like to see them all, but guess I will have a few days off with you people first.

I must stop now.

FIGURE 57: Welcome home button

After the War

Eugene returned home to recover from his illness. Upon recuperation, he entered the University of Syracuse in Architecture. He married Florence ("Flo") Hibbard and had three children; Laura (born 1905), Mary (born 1909) and Russell (born 1910).

Together with a friend, Eugene started an architectural firm. The firm was dissolved in 1916 due to lack of work. Through his friendship with Senator William Calder of New York, he received an administration appointment with the Philadelphia Naval Reserve Fleet. Following WWI, Eugene was hired as the American Tire Chain Company in York, Pa. architect. Eugene died March 6, 1923, at the age of 48.

FIGURE 58: Eugene Hayward Sackett and family, ca. 1914.

References

Faust, Karl Irving
    1899 *Campaigning in the Philippines*. San Francisco: The Hicks-Judd Company.

Karnow, Stanley
    1898 *In Our Image: America's Empire in the Philippines*. New York: Ballantine Books.

Short, First Sergeant Phil. H.
    1899 "Official History f the Operations of the First North Dakota Infantry, U.S.V. in the Campaign in the Philippine Island." In *Campaigning in the Philippines* by Karl Irving Faust, Supplemental Gages 1–19. San Francisco: The Hicks-Judd Company.

Smith, Joseph
    1994 *The Spanish-American War: Conflict in the Caribbean and the Pacific*. London: Longman

Trask, David F.
    1981 *The War with Spain in 1898*. Lincoln: University of Nebraska Press.